759.

110/7/595 Wedding

THE PRINCE OF WALES'S WEDDING

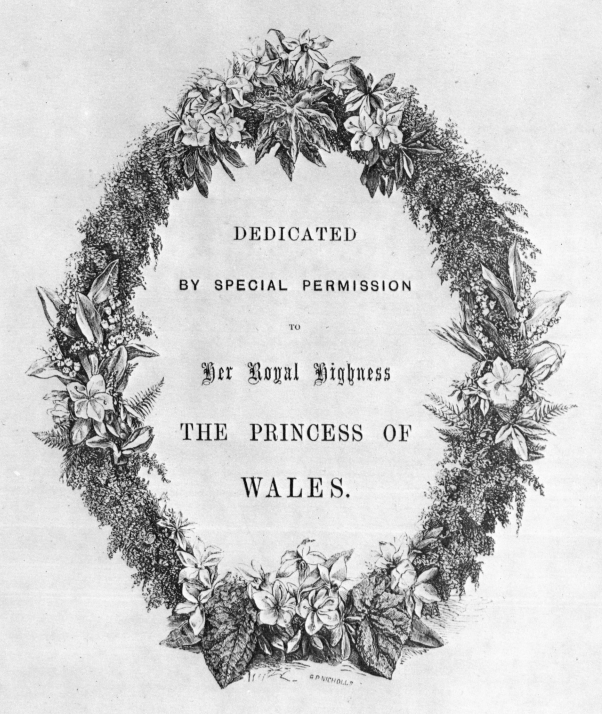

DEDICATED

BY SPECIAL PERMISSION

TO

Her Royal Highness

THE PRINCESS OF

WALES.

G.P. NICHOLLS

Frame of a Mirror, composed of Natural Flowers, placed on the
Toilet Table of the Princess (March 10).

THE PRINCE OF WALES'S WEDDING

The Story of a Picture

JEREMY MAAS

CAMERON & TAYLEUR
in association with
DAVID & CHARLES

Published by Cameron & Tayleur (Books) Limited, 25 Lloyd Baker Street, London WC1X 9AT
in association with David & Charles (Publishers) Ltd, Brunel House, Newton Abbot, Devon.
Distributed by David & Charles (Publishers) Ltd.

Setting by Trade Linotype Limited, Railway Terrace, Nechells, Birmingham B7 5NG.
Printing by Page Bros. (Norwich) Limited, Mile Cross Lane, Norwich, Norfolk NOR 45N.
Binding by Robert Hartnoll Limited, Victoria Square, Bodmin, Cornwall.

First published 1977.

Printed and bound in Great Britain.

ISBN 0 7153 7419 2

Designed by Ian Cameron.

Frontispiece:
Dedication page from 'The Wedding at Windsor, A Memorial of the Marriage of H.R.H. Albert Edward Prince of Wales and H.R.H. Alexandra Princess of Denmark' by W. H. Russell, published by Day and Son, London, Lithographers to the Queen and H.R.H. the Prince of Wales.

CONTENTS

THE ENGAGEMENT

On 25th January 1858, the eldest of Queen Victoria's nine children, the Princess Royal, was married in the Chapel Royal, St James's, to Prince Frederick William of Prussia. Eighteen years before, the Queen herself had been married to Prince Albert of Saxe-Coburg-Gotha in the very same place that her 'darling Flower' now knelt. At the ceremony was a daunting array of Prince Frederick's Hohenzollern relatives, among whom some of the younger princes, tall, ferociously moustached and much given to martial posturing, were a source of some discomfort to the Queen.

As the Princess Royal knelt beside her groom, an artist was busy making sketches of the scene. It was this exact moment that was intended for a finished picture of the ceremony. The artist was the Scots-born John Phillip, then a mere Associate of the Royal Academy, but one who had already been patronized by the Queen and Prince Consort. Phillip was one of the few British artists at that time who had demonstrated an ability, at least in his Spanish pictures (some of which the Queen had bought) to compose convincing crowd scenes, while at the same time capturing likenesses.

But 'Spanish' Phillip was hardly an obvious choice for such a commission, since there was another artist whose credentials far outweighed his own. This was his friend William Powell Frith, whose *Ramsgate Sands* the Queen had bought in 1854 for a thousand guineas. This crowded and colourful picture was Frith's first great popular success and held promise of similar ventures from the brush of one who was not averse to being guided by opportunism.

Frith had been born in 1819, the same year as the Queen; his father was the landlord of the Dragon Hotel, Harrogate. On leaving school, he narrowly escaped becoming an auctioneer, finally becoming a painter. ('He must have tossed up,' James McNeill Whistler concluded on reading of this in Frith's memoirs). While still a student at the Schools of the Royal Academy, he began portrait painting. Later, through the influence of an uncle who ran an hotel in Brook Street, Mayfair, he began a thriving practice of portrait painting among the gentlemen farmers of Lincolnshire who paid five pounds for a head, ten for a kit-cat (less than

Victoria, Crown Princess of Prussia, Princess Royal. *Carte-de-visite* photograph by Helm. Graf, Berlin. All the *carte-de-visite* photographs reproduced in this book, except for that of Frith himself, are taken from the album of photographs used by the artist in the painting of the Wedding Picture.

William Powell Frith R.A., photographed by Maull & Polyblank, London.

half-length) and fifteen for a half-length – always life-size. In 1840, he exhibited his first subject pictures (illustrating Shakespeare) at the Royal Academy. In 1845 he was elected A.R.A., becoming a full Academician in 1853, filling the vacancy caused by the death of Turner.

With the notable exception of the *Dolly Varden* pictures of the early 1840s, Frith had hesitated to attempt subjects in 'unpicturesque' contemporary dress, so the happy idea, which occurred to him during his summer holiday of 1851 at Ramsgate, of trying his hand at modern dress lent his career an entirely new impetus and direction. Without forsaking his continued treatment of subjects from Shakespeare, Scott, Dickens, Sterne and other authors, he now embarked on a series of large-scale compositions of contemporary life. In 1856 he exhibited *Many Happy Returns of the Day*, a particularly felicitous picture in sharp, vibrant colours. This painting, together with its attendant engraving, was eventually to advance his reputation still further. And with every success, Frith's self-confidence (never truly in danger of being in short supply) increased by leaps and bounds.

Initial critical reaction to *The Birthday*, as the artist called it, had, however, been tepid, with some critics detecting a great falling off since *Ramsgate Sands*, and even asserting that he was 'done for'. Frith himself was perfectly content with the 'execution of the picture' and, moreover, knew very well that *The Birthday* could not possibly have 'offered opportunity for the display of character and variety of incident that distinguished the *Sands*.'

Two years earlier, though, he had detected just such an opportunity, which resulted in his best known picture. In 1854, he witnessed his first major race-meeting at Hampton, where he conceived the idea of depicting a great horse-race on canvas. It was not until 1856 that he went to the Derby and shortly afterwards made his first sketches. These were followed by a 'small careful oil-sketch'. Jacob Bell, the pharmacist and patron of artists, had asked Frith to paint an important picture for him as soon as he had found a subject agreeable to both artist and patron. On seeing the sketch for *The Derby Day*, he promptly commissioned the artist to 'paint a picture, five or six feet long from it, at the price of fifteen hundred pounds.' Before the picture was even begun, the copyright for the engraving had been sold to Ernest Gambart, the great print-publisher and dealer, for another £1,500. Throughout 1857 and the early months of 1858, Frith worked incessantly on *The Derby Day*, and as the picture progressed, so he noticed that his confidence was in danger of merging into conceit.

Subject-conscious painters like Frith were intensely jealous for their offspring and would even avoid each other in the street in order not to divulge accidentally the subjects of their latest pictures. So it is hardly likely that Queen Victoria knew of his intentions in July 1857, when she commanded the Keeper of the Privy Purse, Sir Charles Phipps, who was also Private Secretary to the Prince Consort (and a man of integrity and zeal), to ascertain whether Mr Frith might be agreeable to paint a group from the ceremony of the marriage of the Princess Royal. Phipps wrote to Frith on 31st July 1857, and put the question, adding that, in the event of his undertaking the commission, the painter was to keep himself 'disengaged for the purpose' and, at the same time, asking him for some idea of 'the cost of such a picture'.

Frith, who rarely shrank from self-praise, could hardly have failed to interpret these overtures as a compliment to his artistic talent, particularly as they issued from the royal presence. He may well have relished the quandary in which he now found himself. Tempting though such an honour must have been, he made his excuses. 'The "command" surprised me in the act of finishing *The Derby Day*,' he later wrote with some exaggeration, 'and I was permitted to urge the claims of that work, and its owners, as an excuse for declining a task afterwards so ably performed by my friend Phillip.'

Ever a pragmatic man, Frith would have been only too well aware of the snares of official painting. Many a promising artistic career, caught in its coils, had been stifled by it. Frith would surely have known of the tragic fate of the talented painter Luke Clennell, who had been commissioned by the Earl of Bridgwater to paint a large picture of the allied sovereigns at the civic banquet at the Guildhall in 1814. He was at once engulfed in difficulties: even when he was able to obtain sittings for portraits, he quickly fell victim to the arrogance, vanity and caprice of his sitters. When he was at last able to complete a sketch and, three years later, to proceed with work on his large picture, his mind suddenly went blank. To the astonishment of his friends, who had had no previous warning, he became insane. Twenty-three years later, he died in a lunatic asylum in Newcastle-upon-Tyne.

The appalling example of Sir George Hayter, who was still alive and held the appointment of Painter in Ordinary and Painter of History and Portraits in the Queen's Household, should also have been a sufficient deterrent. Once a spirited painter of some promise, he had, in the words of the Countess of Blessington, been a victim of 'the calamity of artists who have been early patronised by great personages to abandon Nature in her simple forms and humble aspects, for subjects appertaining to state ceremonials, court pageants, or Royal progresses, suggested by courtiers or commanded by sovereigns or their consorts.' She added caustically that 'Sir George Hayter has been much patronised by the Queen and Prince Albert.' Indeed, one of Hayter's duties had been to paint the ceremony of the Queen's own wedding to the Prince Consort at the Chapel Royal in 1840. Apparently intimidated by what appears to have been a rather intimate family occasion, Hayter painted with a lack of gusto that made his figures look stiff and starched.

To be fair, one must admit that it was not always so. Winterhalter thrived within the confines of courtly patronage throughout Europe, and his ordinary subject pictures in no way suggest the suppression of an otherwise virile talent. G. H. Thomas was an artist little known outside the royal family, except as an illustrator. As a chronicler of royal and national events, he made sketches which are among the best in the royal collection, inviting comparison (in another field) with the highly accomplished interiors of Joseph Nash. Other artists like William Simpson, Carl Haag and Louis Haghe also did some of their most spirited work under the patronage of the Queen and Prince Consort.

As the year 1858 approached, Frith was well on the way to a crucial stage in his career. It was becoming apparent to those fortunate enough to see the picture in his studio that *The Derby Day* was certain to be a phenomenal success, as indeed it proved to be at the Royal Academy Summer Exhibition of that year. So eagerly did the crowd press forward to see it that, for the safety of the picture, a stout iron rail was placed around it, for the first time since Sir David Wilkie's *Chelsea Pensioners* had been shown there. On that memorable occasion, in 1822, Frith commented, 'thirteen of the elderly Academicians took to their beds in fits of bile and envy; and though a few recovered by steadily refusing medicine, they never were in good health afterwards.' When they visited the exhibition, the Queen and Prince Consort made straight for *The Derby Day*. After a while, the Queen sent for Frith and complimented him 'in the highest and kindest manner'. She said, Frith later recalled, that 'it "was a wonderful work", and much more that modesty prevents my repeating.'
Prince Albert, doubtless stabbing the air with a sharp instrument he invariably kept in his pocket, indicated to Frith certain changes which might be made to improve the picture and surprised the artist by his intimate knowledge of what Frith could only call the *conduct* of a picture. Frith complied with several of the Prince's suggestions, to the great benefit, he claimed, of his work.
The Derby Day sealed Frith's reputation. Its purchase by Jacob Bell, its gift to the nation on his death soon after, its engraving by Auguste Blanchard, the publication of the print by Gambart and subsequent tours of the picture round the world confirmed and spread his renown.

In 1861, Edward, Prince of Wales, was in search of a wife; or rather, his parents (who regarded an early marriage as a panacea for his wayward character), his family and certain sections of the British public were looking for a wife for *him*. It was no easy matter, nor was it made any easier when the Prince of Wales declared flatly that he would marry only for love. His father at once began to compile lists of eligible names. He was soon dismayed, however, to find that there was an alarming shortage of protestant princesses who were neither unprepossessing nor too old. Public opinion was insistent on marriage within the royal caste, and 'The Times', in an attempt to clarify everyone's thoughts, compiled a sonorous short list of nubile princesses. 'To all present appearances,' the Thunderer declaimed, 'our future monarch's choice of a wife is positively limited to exactly seven ladies of the blood-royal, unless, indeed, he selects a consort much older than himself: (1) Princess Alexandrina, daughter of Prince Albert of Prussia; (2) Princess Anna of Hesse-Darmstadt, niece of the Grand Duke of Hesse, and of the Empress of Russia; (3) Princess Augusta of Holstein-Glücksburg; (4) Duchess Wilhelmina of Württemberg; (5) Princess Alexandra, daughter of Prince Christian of Denmark; (6) Princess Mary of Saxe-Altenburg; (7) Princess Catharine of Oldenburg, sister of the Grand Duchess Nicholas of Russia.'

Photographs of princesses were eagerly sought, scrutinized by the Queen and Prince Albert and shown to the Prince of Wales. Deep was their disappointment when he refused to look twice at photographs of a promising discovery, the nineteen-year-old Elizabeth of Wied, who later became Queen of Rumania. With some reluctance, Queen Victoria resigned herself to considering a beautiful but obscure schoolgirl from

Prince Christian of Denmark and his family—Princess Alexandra is on the right. (Royal Library, Copenhagen)

Princess Alexandra photographed by Hermann Ohm, Copenhagen.

Copenhagen. She was number five on 'The Times's' list and her full name was Princess Alexandra Caroline Marie Charlotte Louise Julie of Schleswig-Holstein-Sonderburg-Glücksburg. At first, the Queen viewed the prospects of a Danish marriage with some misgivings; she was prejudiced against the girl's parents, and then there was the Schleswig-Holstein dispute between Prussia and Denmark, a matter of serious concern and baffling complexity. Only three people had ever understood it, as Palmerston was later to remark. One was Prince Albert and he was dead. Another was a German professor and he had gone mad. He, Palmerston, was the third and he had forgotten all about it. This smouldering and dangerous dispute would complicate a rather delicate diplomatic situation if Edward and Alexandra were to marry. It was to cast a deep shadow over all that ensued between Frith and the courts of Europe.

Notwithstanding Queen Victoria's sympathies with the Prussians in the Schleswig-Holstein question and her reservations about Princess Alexandra's family, news that the Emperor Alexander II of Russia had procured photographs of the Princess and had shown them to his eldest son spurred her into speedy activity on behalf of her own son and heir. Photographs were at once obtained and shown to the Prince of Wales, who was informed by his father that, if he were interested, all diplomatic and family objections would be overcome. The Prince was evidently so impressed by the photographs that a secret meeting was arranged. They were presented to each other by the Crown Princess of Prussia at the altar of St Bernard in the cathedral of Speyer in Germany on 24th September 1861, and they met again in Heidelberg on the next day.

After some slight initial thoughts that she did not quite live up to her photographs and that 'her nose was too long and her forehead too low,' the Prince of Wales expressed himself well pleased with her, although, as the Queen noted, he 'seemed nervous about deciding anything yet.' For a while, little happened; the Prince resumed his studies at Cambridge. While on a visit to him there, Prince Albert caught a chill. Typhoid ensued, and he died at Windsor on 14th December 1861, plunging the Queen into the deepest of sorrows and her court into mourning.

With unfailing fidelity to his memory, the Queen resolved to carry out two plans which Albert had devised for his son. The first was a tour of the Holy Land, which was duly made; by June 1862, the Prince of Wales was back at Windsor. The second plan was his engagement to Princess Alexandra. Accordingly, a long continental tour was projected with complicated arrangements for a further meeting with the Danish Princess. Queen Victoria, travelling as *la Comtesse de Balmoral*, stayed with her Uncle Leopold, King of the Belgians, at the Palace of Laeken near Brussels until 4th September, when she left to spend six weeks in Coburg. The Prince of Wales met Princess Alexandra on 5th September at Ostend, where she stayed while he went on to a hotel in Brussels.

The Prince of Wales, Princess Alexandra and her family. (Royal Library, Copenhagen)

From there, he drove every day to Laeken. On the 8th, he was joined by the Princess and other members of the Danish royal family. The following day, the couple were summoned by King Leopold. At Laeken, the Prince of Wales offered Princess Alexandra his hand and heart, and was promptly accepted. On the 16th, the engagement was made public, to the wildest of rejoicings; and, on 1st November, the Queen, grievously lamenting the death of her own husband, gave formal assent to her son's union with the Danish Princess at a meeting of the Privy Council.

FRITH STATES HIS TERMS

In March 1862, Frith had completed the last of his three great scenes from contemporary life, *The Railway Station*. The picture had been commissioned by the florid and vulgar Louis Victor Flatow, a picture dealer, who, despite his deplorable appearance and manner, was much esteemed by Frith and his family, who detected in him not only lovable qualities but quite outstanding business acumen. The price paid for it was £4,500, to include the sketch and copyright, and Frith later resigned his right (and, arguably, his duty as a Royal Academician) to exhibit it at the Royal Academy for a further consideration of £750. Its exhibition at Flatow's private gallery and the subsequent engraving contributed yet more leaves to Frith's garland of laurels.

It was probably the rivalry that existed between Flatow and the rather more successful Ernest Gambart, coupled with the great success attendant upon his modern life subjects, that enabled Frith to obtain from Gambart a commission of enormous magnitude, not to say munificence. By an agreement dated 29th August 1862, Frith was to paint three pictures in which the figures 'shall not be of a less size than the figures in the Picture . . . called *The Railway Station*,' and the series was to be entitled *The Streets of London*. Frith made no secret of his delight in this generous commission, taking care in his reminiscences to insist that the fee was offered, not demanded. The delightful prospect of 'trying to realize all that these subjects were capable of, no tongue can tell,' he wrote, and he completed three sketches, one for each picture, from which it can be seen that they held as much promise as he had clearly anticipated.

The year dawned darkly for the widowed Queen, 'Another year begun in my sorrow and loneliness!' she wrote in her Journal, 'May God help me on! It no longer means anything to me, no fresh chapter of life, – nothing!' Inexorably, however, the affairs of family and state forced themselves on her attention. Absorbed though she was in her grief, the impending marriage needed much thought and preparation. It was to be a grand occasion, which would need to be suitably recorded. And there was one artist pre-eminently qualified to manipulate a huge throng of people on canvas. Doubtless confident that she would not be refused a second time, the Queen let it be known that she wished Frith to paint a picture of the ceremony.

Accordingly feelers were put out. The Queen's Resident Bedchamber Woman, Lady Augusta Bruce, was sent to sound out the views of the President of the Royal Academy, Sir Charles Eastlake. Lady Augusta's soundings were swiftly followed up in a letter on 11th January 1863 from Sir Charles Phipps, the Keeper of the Privy Purse. 'The first thing,' he wrote to Eastlake, 'is to ascertain whether he would be willing and able to undertake it and the second to arrange the terms.' Probably well aware that Frith, like most leading subject painters of the time, would be much concerned with engraving possibilities and copyrights, the letter dwelt at some length on what to a layman could be a wearisome, even an unnecessarily obtrusive subject. Sir Charles wished to convey the Queen's stipulation that the copyright should be vested in the artist, but that the picture might be exhibited only in London, 'for the purpose of obtaining subscribers to the engraving,' and not in the provinces because of the dangers to which prolonged display might expose the picture, not to mention its protracted absence from the Queen. Finally Sir Charles hoped that Eastlake might take over the negotiations, pleading comparative ignorance 'of the ways of the profession.'

Events now moved swiftly. On the evening of 13th January 1863, Frith received a letter from Eastlake 'to say the Queen wished me to paint the Marriage of the Prince of Wales.' This time Frith felt he must obey. He might have been excused had he felt that the subject might perhaps have its own rewards. It can hardly have been mere coincidence that both Hayter and Landseer had not only both been in close proximity to royalty, but had also received knighthoods and the consequent assurance of continued patronage. But first Gambart had to be squared. The publisher was strongly averse to attempts by artists to renege on contracts, whatever the reason, but he always softened perceptibly where the interests of royalty were concerned. Besides, he would have been astute enough to have sensed a means of turning the situation to his advantage. Only a few weeks before, the firm of E. Gambart & Co. had announced the publication of the engraving by Blanchard of *The Marriage of H.R.H. The Princess Royal* after John Phillip.

Gambart called on Frith on 18th January and, according to the artist, 'agreed to the postponement of the street pictures in consequence of the Queen's wish.' Relieved, for the time being, of his commitment to Gambart, Frith now felt free to write to Eastlake, to whom, in a letter dated 19th January, he conveyed his willingness to paint the picture and, assuming that it was to be 'sufficiently large to embrace the whole ceremonial,' that it could not be done in less than a year of actual work and that his 'terms would be three thousand pounds.'

'In fixing that sum I have been entirely influenced by a calculation of the value of my time, being very careful that in the event of my terms being agreeable to the Queen, Her Majesty should pay *less*, rather than *more*, than I can earn by my ordinary practice.' It seems that Gambart, who was personally acquainted with the Queen, had made some kind of application to her, probably in connection with the copyright. This application, Frith assured Eastlake, 'was made without my knowledge and I think a satisfactory arrangement can be made as to the copyright if Her Majesty will allow a reduced copy to be made of the picture.' In conclusion, Frith added that 'if I am entrusted to paint the picture, I will devote myself to it with all my heart.'

Eastlake passed the artist's letter to Phipps on the same day, adding that 'Mr Frith's chief question was whether the entire scene, as an historical subject, was desired, or only some episode in it' – and that Frith had assumed that the picture was to commemorate the entire subject, otherwise, he might have added, why approach the master of crowd scenes in the first place?

In a letter three days later, Phipps was able to tell Eastlake that 'The Queen did not want . . . so comprehensive a picture as Mr Frith seems to contemplate.' The wedding was to take place at the St George's Chapel, Windsor, and Frith might like to 'see the locality and then judge what he could do.' Her Majesty clearly wanted a rather intimate picture, such as Phillip had painted.

Frith's mounting impatience with the tortuous method of communication used by the participants at these early stages must have provoked him to some kind of protest, since Eastlake, in a letter to him on 24th January, felt constrained to issue a mild rebuke and a plea for compliance, at least temporarily, with the cumbersome arrangement. In short, Frith was asked not to correspond directly with Phipps, but to continue using

Part of letter from Sir Charles Eastlake to Frith, 24th January 1863.

Eastlake as intermediary. At last, Eastlake could give him an approximate date for the wedding and tell him that preparations were already begun in the chapel. If Frith wanted to see for himself, he had only to consult Mr Seabrook, Inspector at Windsor Castle.

It seems that Frith was far from happy with the situation, and it is likely that rumours had reached him of dismay in high places at the price he was asking; nor was consideration of an engraving of the picture far from his thoughts when he wrote to Eastlake on 26th January:

'I have reflected a good deal on the proposal that I should paint an episode of the Marriage of the Prince of Wales & I have come to the conclusion that I could neither do myself nor the subject justice by such a method of treatment, my reputation would suffer by a comparison with the works of other painters of similar subjects whose efforts have remained unfettered, & an engraving would be rendered doubtful if not altogether nugatory, in its result, by such restricted conditions.

'I still venture to hope that the Queen will permit me to endeavour to realize so great a scene in my own way. Unless this can be conceded to me, I must resign the enviable task to some other hand & I need scarcely say with how much regret I should see so remarkable an opportunity of distinguishing myself pass away.

'It has occurred to me that the price I have asked may appear so large as to require some explanation & at the risk of being tedious I will trouble you with a few words on the subject.

'In the matter of mere remuneration the sum I received for the picture of *The Railway Station* far exceeded that which I feel justified in asking for the proposed picture of the Marriage of the Prince of Wales, & at this moment there is secured to me by a legal document the sum of ten thousand pounds for three pictures the painting of which cannot occupy me longer than two years.

'Under these circumstances I submit that I have fixed a fair price for so laborious a subject as the Marriage of the Prince of Wales – I solicit an early reply.'

The artist rarely made copies of his own letters. On this occasion he did.

Eastlake passed Frith's letter to Phipps with scarcely a comment, observing, merely, that the transactions of publishers (like Gambart), on whom artists were in great measure and not unwillingly dependent, were then so gigantic that it seemed 'difficult to make arrangements with artists without their intervention.'

Frith's letter was a bold stroke, and it achieved the desired effect, for on the very next day Phipps wrote to Eastlake that 'the Queen had not desired so large a picture as Mr Frith appears to contemplate but H.M. would not wish to restrict (further than is absolutely necessary) Mr Frith in his mode of treating the subject proposed to him, still less would H.M. desire that any diminution should be made of the remuneration which he considered sufficient for his time & the exercise of his skill.

'The Queen would therefore authorize you to assent to Mr Frith's

Retraction printed in The 'Art-Journal'
for March 1863.

proposal – but H.M. would wish to see you after Her arrival at Windsor, to arrange with regard to the size & shape of the proposed picture.'

Two days later, a triumphant Frith wrote in his diary: 'Sir C. Phipps writes to say the Queen agrees to my terms for the Marriage of the Prince of Wales – three thousand pounds.'

Almost at once the decision was made public. The Queen's acceptance of Frith's terms came too late to save the artist from a ferocious attack in the February issue of 'The Art-Journal'. Its editor, S. C. Hall, a self-appointed guardian of the morality of artists and dealers alike, accused Frith, without actually naming him, of asking a 'preposterous sum' for the picture, adding that 'his "terms" were declined, and rightly.' He was sure, among other things, that 'there are English painters better qualified to produce a work for which the subjects are furnished by the court and aristocracy of Great Britain, and not by the railroad and the race-course.'

Frith forced Hall to make an apology; this made its oleaginous appearance in the next issue, together with a statement that Frith's terms had been 'acceded to in the most gracious and liberal manner.' A corrected proof remained in Frith's possession until his death.

Some years after the Queen's death, Frith's daughter, Mrs Panton, made some revealing comments on the commission. She could never understand, she wrote, 'why in those days the royal folk always paid less for their pictures than any one else . . . I am sure my father lost hundreds of pounds over the picture of the Marriage . . . and what it cost him in wear and tear of nerves, time and temper, no one will ever know. Of course he gave a guarded description of his doings with the Royalties in his own book of Reminiscences: I only wish he had told them at length, but in those days Queen Victoria was still alive, and he had actually to submit his proof sheets to her before the book was published!'

Frith, in fact, devoted an entire chapter to his painting of the Royal Wedding in the first volume of his autobiography, published in 1887. Happily, the survival of the papers concerned with the picture makes it possible, using the chapter as framework, to reconstruct the events with a frankness denied, alas – for he was an inimitable raconteur – to Frith.

Almost immediately after agreement had been reached with the Queen, even Frith, veteran of the crowded canvas, was filled with mis-givings. 'I was aware,' he later recalled, 'of the fearful difficulties that such a subject presented – scarcely exaggerated by what Landseer said to me when he heard of my temerity: "So you are going to do the marriage picture? Well for all the money in this world, and all in the next, I wouldn't undertake such a thing." Not much appalled by this and other warnings, undertake it I did; and the street scenes, for which I was to receive the incredible sum of ten thousand pounds from Mr. Gambart . . . were put on one side.' These street scenes, so absolutely within the compass of Frith's own special talent, were, except as minor sketches, never painted.

BATTLE ROYAL

In early 1863, while Civil War raged in America and the tiresome Schleswig-Holstein dispute continued to smoulder on the Continent, England basked in tranquil prosperity. And, as public enthusiasm for the impending marriage grew warmer every day, so relations between Germany and Denmark grew cooler. Although the British government attached no political significance to the marriage, the Prussians could not help seeing it as a slight, in spite of Queen Victoria's sympathy with their cause, while the Danes, in their turn, could not but see anything in it but auguries hopeful for themselves.

Preparations for the royal wedding now went ahead with increasing vigour. As far as Frith was concerned, for the moment all that mattered was what *shape* his picture should be. Portrait or landscape shaped? Upright or oblong? It all came to the same thing – high or long? There is no doubt which shape Frith favoured – long. Apart from the inescapable fact that weddings were by their nature latitudinal, so also were all crowd scenes, at least those that Frith had so far painted. But, for reasons which will become apparent, the Queen favoured the upright shape.

Then there was the fraught question of the size of the figures – not only in relation to the size of the picture, but to each other and to the overall shape. Again it fell to the lot of the President of the Royal Academy to help decide the issue with Queen Victoria. Accordingly, on 12th February, Sir Charles Eastlake, equipped with a two-foot rule, was granted an audience with the Queen. Also present to help solve the vexatious problem were her daughter Princess Alice and son-in-law Prince Louis of Hesse-Darmstadt.

Frith had previously apprised Eastlake of his wish to paint the foreground figures twenty-two inches high, on a canvas measuring six to eight feet across. Indicating with his rule, Eastlake was able to give some idea of Frith's scheme. After consulting the Prince and Princess, the Queen said that she could see no objection to the height of the foreground figures, nor even to the 'proposed extent of the picture', so long as Mr Frith could 'comprehend the part of the chapel, above', where she herself would be placed. This consideration was 'so important as to make it a question whether the picture should not be high rather than long.'

Writing to Frith on the same day, Eastlake told him that the Queen had suggested that since it was she herself who had thought of it as a high, rather than a long, picture, 'whether the architecture might not in that case be important.' Unfortunately Eastlake could remember little of the architectural details of St Georges Chapel, Windsor; nor could he imagine where the Queen was to be placed, and could not, therefore, advise Frith on the point. Did Mr Frith know, perhaps?

The Queen had decided to play her part in the ceremony from the royal closet which overlooks the high altar from the north side of the choir. Such elevation would certainly focus attention as much on the architectural details as on the nearest of her relations in the scene below, less important guests thus being totally excluded from the picture. Perhaps she saw this as a kinder fate than being reduced to one of a sea of featureless blobs in a long picture such as Frith hoped to paint.

It was now that Frith hit upon a plan to show the force of his arguments, by offering to submit to Her Majesty two sketches, one treating it 'as a high picture, the other treating it in length.' On 14th February Eastlake conveyed Frith's wish to the Queen, who 'quite approved' of his having 'come to this conclusion'. Whose views prevailed in this difference of opinion may be determined from the eventual shape of the picture – long: ten feet long, in fact.

Frith next turned his attention to photographic aids. In the very infancy of photography, nearly eleven years before, he had attempted its use as an aid in painting *Ramsgate Sands*, but without success. He had used it successfully to assist him in the painting of *The Derby Day*. As the day of the wedding neared, Frith realized that on such a transitory occasion photography would be more useful than ever before. Accordingly, he approached Mr Window, partner in the photographic portrait business of Window and Bridge, of Baker Street.

Window was asked to submit a plan to Frith for securing likenesses of the royal couple with the least inconvenience to them. His plan was simple, although hardly so by modern standards. Surmising that photographs taken before or after the event would be of less value than those taken on the day of the wedding, when 'emotions . . . naturally kindle a thousand traits which cannot be put on again with the wedding dress,' he proposed to erect a 'temporary glass house against some doorway near to which Their Royal Highnesses will have to pass, and from the earliest possible moment for their arrival until they actually come, to keep a constant relay of sensitive plates ready so that on their arrival nothing will have to be done but to pose them and to expose the plates.'

By this means, Window estimated that he could take three photographs of the royal couple (two posed separately and one of them together) in ten minutes. If only one were required, he could manage it in less than two minutes. He intended to work with two cameras simultaneously taking both a large and a small full-length portrait with each exposure. The photographs of the bride's father, Prince Christian, a

Prince Christian of Denmark.

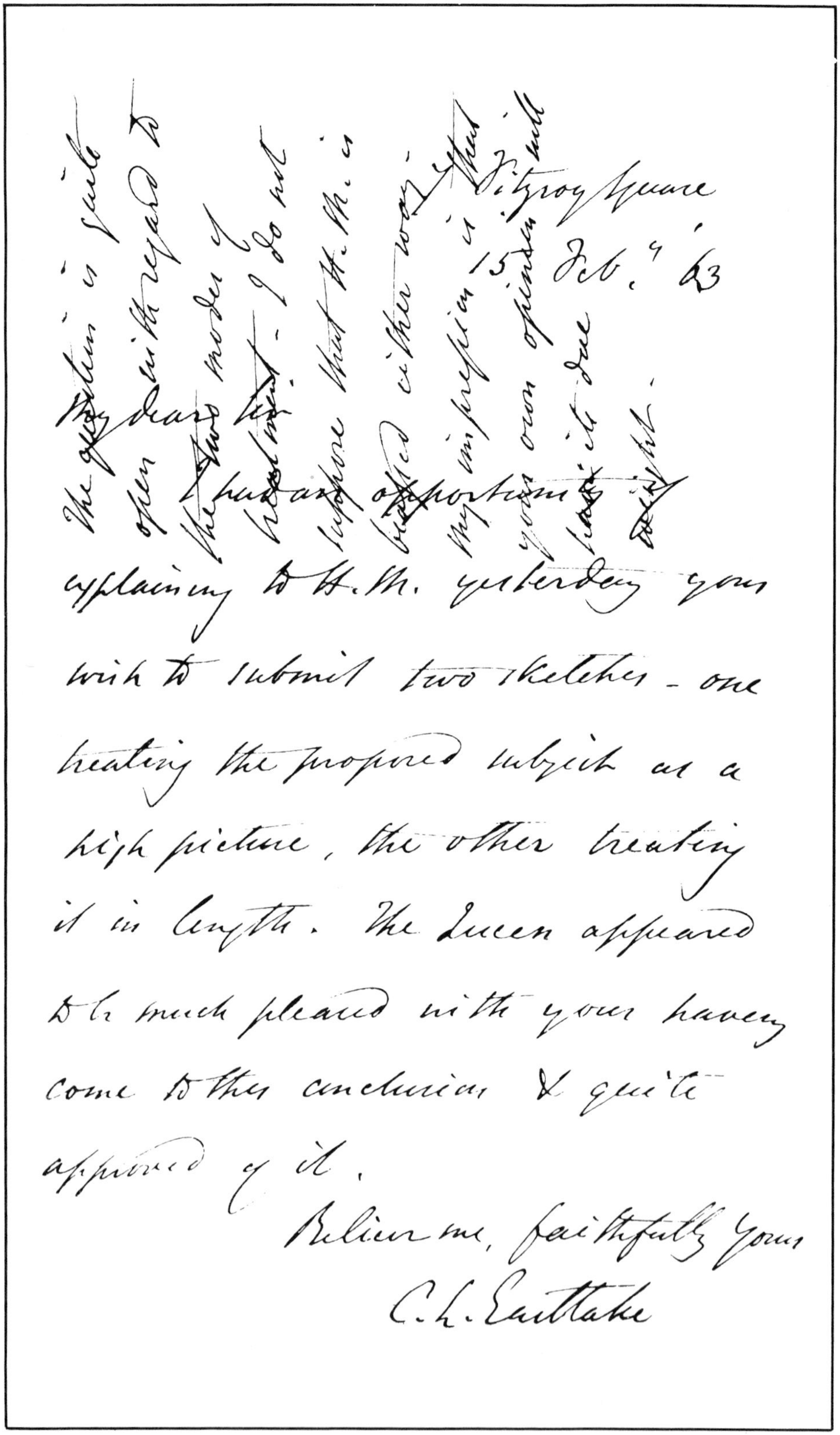

7 Fitzroy Square
15 Feby 63

My dear Sir

I had an opportunity of explaining to H.M. yesterday your wish to submit two sketches - one treating the proposed subject as a high picture, the other treating it in length. The Queen appeared to be much pleased with your having come to this conclusion & quite approved of it.

The question is quite open with regard to the two modes of treatment - I do not suppose that H.M. is pledged either way - that impression is your own opinion will leave it free [illegible]

Believe me, faithfully yours
C. L. Eastlake

Letter from Sir Charles Eastlake to Frith, 15th February 1863.

poor but estimable man who lived on his pay as an officer in the Danish Guards, could be taken at some future date in Window's studio, together with those of other members of the Danish royal family, whose stay in London would be short.

Window set out his battle plan in a letter to Frith on the 26th. As time was running short, Frith endorsed Window's letter with his own comments and forwarded it to Eastlake, who, if he thought it proper, was to 'lay it before the Queen – only observing that I shall be quite content that the photographs be taken as Her Majesty proposes.'

So far, the exchanges between Frith, Phipps, Eastlake and the Queen had had an air of leisurely cordiality with only a rare hint, now and then, of scarcely contained fractiousness below the surface. But now all this was to change. Eastlake's reply to Frith, written on the same day, contained two bombshells, which detonated with considerable force when Frith read the letter at his house in Bayswater. The effect of the first was immediate; the second burned with a slower fuse.

Eastlake was unable to pass Window's letter (with Frith's comments) to Phipps who was attending one of the innumerable levées, but gave it 'with due explanations to Lady Augusta Bruce . . . requesting her to see the Queen on the subject.' Shortly after the Queen had been acquainted with Window's proposals, she sent for Eastlake. Mr Window's presence as a photographer at the wedding was out of the question, she told him, although he might photograph the bridal couple 'after their return.' In any case, she had some weeks previously commanded Mr Vernon Heath to take photographs at the wedding; his 'process', she understood, 'was peculiar . . . and likely to be very successful.'

Vernon Heath was a 43-year-old pioneer photographer, the nephew of Robert Vernon, the horse-dealer who had amassed a fortune during the Napoleonic wars by the sale of horses to the army and who was also a notable patron of artists. Heath had earned a special place in the Queen's priorities by having taken the last photograph of the Prince Consort. He was to pursue a strikingly uneventful career, during the course of which he gave photographic lessons to Prince Alfred and Dr Livingstone. His career was nearly terminated at the age of seventy-two, when, owing his landlord fourteen weeks' rent and having been evicted two days previously, he was charged with attempting to commit suicide by walking into the Thames at East Molesey. His defence that he fell into the water because the bank gave way earned him a discharge on the promise that he would go back to his friends. In this same year, Heath published his recollections, which afford a rare insight into the early use of photographs on a ceremonial occasion.

Unknown to Frith, Heath had probably started his photographic experiments in St George's Chapel by 26th February. Day by day, he experimented with his cumbersome apparatus until 'such a result was arrived at, that I felt justified in reporting that providing the day was fairly fine, there was a probability that I might be successful.'

The second bombshell contained in Eastlake's letter was a terse statement that another painter, G. H. Thomas, was also to be present on the great occasion 'to paint a picture, but representing a very different moment – the procession leaving after the ceremony.' *After the ceremony*, he had quite clearly said. Eastlake ended by telling Frith that he was at last at liberty to communicate directly with Phipps 'to save time'.

The news that Thomas, too, was to paint a picture of the wedding was also announced in the March issue of 'The Art-Journal', a page after Hall's apology. The editor was thus able to vent his spleen by declaring that 'there is no artist better calculated to do justice to a subject so deeply interesting.'

In those days, artists were inordinately touchy not only about the subjects of their pictures, but also on the subject of their copyrights. These could be as valuable as pictures themselves where there was the possibility that engraving might be made, and no pains were spared, no quarter given, in efforts to define where a potentially exploitable copyright might exist and to determine its correct assignment. Frith, Gambart, and indeed whole sections of the artistic fraternity and print trade were at that time fighting to clarify the existing copyright laws and to challenge infringements, mainly piracies, in the law courts.

It is hardly surprising, therefore, that Frith, in his first letter to Phipps (27th February) saw fit to fire a heavy salvo on the matter of copyright. It was the first of a series of broadsides which must have astonished the diligent courtier. Of course, he, Mr Frith, could raise no objection to Mr Heath's taking a photograph of the ceremony 'so long as *it is not published*;' nor could he, for that matter, object to any picture or photograph so long as it did not, 'in the eyes of the owner of the copyrights – damage his interests.' All that Frith quite reasonably wanted was a photographic reminiscence of the dresses, ornaments, etc., which were to be worn on that occasion.

There was another matter, too. The Hon. Spencer Ponsonby, Comptroller, Lord Chamberlain's Department, had not even found it possible to promise Frith a place in the chapel with a good view of the ceremony, with the excuse that this decision rested entirely with the Queen. Perhaps Sir Charles could use his influence, Frith suggested. Phipps must eventually have succeeded, as events would show.

There is a note of exasperated resignation in Phipps's reply, made the next day. Frith, it seemed all too clear to him, appeared to believe that he owned the copyright of an ancient and sacred ceremony in which the eldest son of Queen Victoria and heir to the throne of Great Britain and the Empire was the leading participant. The tone of Phipps's letter suggests that such knavish effrontery was scarcely to be endured and must most certainly be corrected.

Phipps, as he told Frith, could not for the life of him see how there could be 'copyright of a Scene or an Event any more than a landscape or

Sir Charles Phipps photographed by John & Charles Watkins, London.

a building.' Indeed, any number of artists, draughtsmen, photographers and the like, whole armies of them, with brushes, palettes, pencils, sketchbooks, easels, wet plate cameras, tripods, portable laboratories, could be swarming all over the same ceremony, without in any way interfering with each other's copyrights. Moreover, 'although the Queen would naturally not order two representations of the same moment of time in a ceremonial such as this marriage,' he could hardly imagine that Her Majesty would allow any attempt, such as Frith's, to 'limit her power to permit' or even to 'order other representations of different periods of time.'

Phipps had no doubt that, while 'every possible facility' would subsequently be afforded Frith for the perfection of his picture, there could be no photographs taken of either bride or groom on the wedding day.

Frith was not to be daunted. On 3rd March, with only a week to go before the wedding, he returned to the attack. In a letter written on that day, Frith agreed that there could be no copyright 'in "a *scene* or an *event*",' but suggested that nevertheless there was a copyright of *both*. And, if there were to be a number of representations of the ceremony, he was 'bound to inform the publisher who may be the possessor of any copyright of such an event.'

What of Eastlake's promise to him of 'the copyright of intended picture'? Were there to be any other artists engaged to paint the ceremony? Beyond being informed that Mr Thomas was to paint the procession leaving the *Chapel*, he had heard no more on the subject.

Frith showed here that either he had misunderstood Eastlake's letter or that, by a cunning interpretation of Eastlake's phrase, he hoped to get Thomas out of the chapel altogether, thus forcing him to paint the scene outside, as the procession left the building. Eastlake had clearly written *after* the ceremony. And it would become clear that he meant while the bridal couple and congregation were still inside the chapel.

Phipps's patience showed signs of rapid evaporation when he replied swiftly on the same day. Perhaps, he wrote, it would be better to 'talk this all over' in two days time, when Frith intended visiting the chapel 'for the purpose of taking a photograph of the interior.' Whatever the outcome of this confrontation, however, Phipps could not resist a telling observation. While he was well aware 'that the representation of the same Scene by many artists would lower the Value of the Copyright of each,' there would still be no infringements, although – and this was the shattering truth, for Frith of all artists knew well the value of a copyright – 'there would doubtless be an interference with the interests of the publisher.'

Phipps must have known very well that if Frith did indeed possess the copyright (that is, if a copyright existed in the first place), then there was perhaps as much as £3,000 to be gained by its sale to a publisher. Gambart had, after all, paid £1,500 for the copyright of *The Derby Day*, not one penny less than Bell had paid for the picture.

As if this were not enough, Phipps had two more uncomfortable items of news for the artist. He was not aware, he told Frith, that the Queen had ordered any other pictures, but he did know that Thomas, besides painting the procession, had been commissioned by Mr Day and Son, Lithographers to the Queen and Prince of Wales, to paint a picture (of the bridal couple kneeling at the altar, as Frith would later learn) *and* make a water-colour drawing for the Prince of Wales.

Part of letter from Sir Charles Phipps to Frith, 3rd March 1863.

THE WEDDING

The wedding was celebrated on Tuesday, 10th March 1863, amid a surge of popular rejoicing. Not since the wedding of the Princess Royal in 1858 had there been such a demonstration of loyal fervour and public gaiety.

To Disraeli it seemed that 'the long-pent-up feeling of affectionate devotion to the Queen, and of sympathy for her sorrows, came out with that deep and fervid enthusiasm for which the people of England are, I think, remarkable.' Although none could doubt the fathomless depths of the Queen's grief, already there were complaints of selfishness in such sorrow. There was even a rumour that she had wished the chapel to be

The Reception of Princess Alexandra at Gravesend, engraved by C. P. Nicholls for 'The Wedding at Windsor'.

TON. Here the most elaborate preparations had been made to receive the Princess with all honour. Every house in the ancient place was illuminated; the outlines of the venerable College were marked out by thousands of lamps; the residences of the Provost and of the Masters were beautifully lighted up, and inscriptions of welcome graced the front of the College buildings. The Volunteer Corps of Eton boys was under arms. Eton did everything that loyalty and good taste could devise to welcome the Royal Bride. Two Triumphal Arches were prepared,—one by the Town of Eton, which is represented in the wood-engraving; the other, which cost £400, was erected by the Etonians, from the designs of Mr. Nash, of the Society of Painters in Water Colours, under whose superintendence it was raised.

hung with black and that the Prince of Wales had retorted, 'Then I'd better bring my bride in a hearse.' Even Palmerston, dismayed that the Queen had appealed to a bust of Prince Albert and then related his reply to the Premier, had said (out of her hearing), 'I will argue this matter with any *live* Prince you like, but hang me if I can manage a dead one.' Nevertheless, there is little doubt that the sombre mood of the Queen lent a certain resonance, a sense of poignancy to an occasion of high-keyed jubilance.

Princess Alexandra had landed at Gravesend three days previously, accompanied by her parents, Prince Christian and Princess Louise, her three brothers, the Princes Frederick, William and Waldemar, and her two sisters, the Princesses Dagmar and Thyra, as well as by her two uncles, the Duke of Holstein-Glücksburg and Prince Frederick of Hesse-Cassel. The scandalously dissolute King of Denmark had not been invited.

The Prince of Wales, who had nearly arrived late at Gravesend,

Engravings:
The Preparations at Eton and the arrival of the Royal Procession at Windsor by C. P. Nicholls for 'The Wedding at Windsor'.
Photograph:
Royal group, taken on 9th March 1863 at Windsor Castle. Left to right: Prince and Princess Christian, Prince Frederick of Denmark, Princess Alice, the Crown Prince of Prussia, Prince Louis of Hesse, Princess Helena, Princess Alexandra, the Prince of Wales, the Crown Princess of Prussia, Princess Dagmar of Denmark, Princess Louise, Prince William of Denmark. (Royal Archives, Windsor Castle)

caused initial astonishment, which quickly turned to a storm of cheers, by greeting the Princess with a kiss in full view of the crowds. The saloon train in which the Princess and her parents had been joined by the Prince of Wales took them to the Bricklayer's Arms Station in Southwark, whence they made their triumphal progress by way of the Temple Bar, Pall Mall, Piccadilly and Hyde Park to Paddington Station. Everywhere they were borne along by a sea of hats, hands and waving white handkerchiefs. One observer, Henry Silver of 'Punch', was amazed to see that the British populace had so many white handkerchiefs. The progress through the city was marred by the incompetence of the police, who had to beat back the exuberant crowds, whirling their truncheons, cracking skulls left and right. The Princess visibly shuddered as the carriage wheels almost grazed the front ranks of the crowds; there were faces streaming with blood and people screaming for mercy. So thick was the throng at one point that it had to be dispersed by a charge of the Life Guards with sabres drawn.

Their train took the royal party from Paddington to Slough, where another procession formed and drove to Windsor. At Eton, passing through two triumphal arches in the pouring rain, the couple were cheered lustily by the schoolboys. On their arrival at Windsor, they were met by the Queen, who, after the excitement of the greetings, felt too 'desolate' to appear at dinner.

The Wedding Morning

BOROUGH OF WINDSOR has not been spoiled by its long contact with Royalty, but it is usually not so demonstrative in its rejoicings as less favoured places. However, on this occasion, there was an energy in decoration, and in all the steps taken to prepare for the Wedding, which left nothing to be desired.

On 9th March, the day before the wedding, while the finishing touches were being put to St George's Chapel and guests arrived at the castle, the Queen took the engaged couple into the Mausoleum at Frogmore, where the Prince Consort was buried. Joining their hands together, she took them both in her arms. In a moment that touched them all, the Queen announced: '*He* gives you his blessing!'

At sunrise on the morning of 10th March, the Royal Standard was, in the words of W. H. Russell, 'flung to the frosty air.' Already the streets of Windsor, decorated with triumphal arches, streamers and wreaths, were milling with excited crowds. At eight o'clock, the bells of Windsor began to peal; their sound mingled with the shouting of orders, the jingling of armour and clatter of horses as the troops took up their positions. The throng began to be flecked with bright uniforms and flashing breast-plates. The sound of bells was shortly joined by the thunder of cannon, as though to remind the common folk (if reminder were needed) that this was no ordinary occasion.

Just after ten o'clock, all was ready. Special platforms outside the chapel were filled, and all the spectators could do was wait, whiling away the time by noting every little incident that caught the eye. Carriage after carriage rattled over the crisp, frozen gravel, bringing guests to the chapel; some six hundred to the nave, and a privileged two hundred who were to be crowded into the choir, in the permanent stalls and on specially constructed tiers and platforms. Among those to arrive was William Powell Frith.

Reception and martialling areas, robing and dressing-rooms, as well as all the impedimenta of pageantry were housed in a temporary building erected against the west door of the chapel. It was designed as a vast Gothic hall, so large that the centre section held a medieval banqueting hall. From this temporary building many of the guests and functionaries passed through the west door into the nave or further on into the choir.

It was from this door, too, that, shortly before eleven o'clock, there emerged into the chapel a pack apparently of playing-card figures, straight from Wonderland: the Garter King-at-Arms, attired in a crimson satin mantle and carrying a sceptre, accompanied by Clarenceux and Norroy, and followed by a pomp of Heralds, Pursuivants, Trumpeters and Drummers. With suitable dignity, they all took up their allotted positions.

It was not until half past eleven that the full state ceremony began. Queen Victoria, shy of public glare, made her way privately to the chapel, where she was received by the Lord Chamberlain and conducted with her attendants to her chosen place. Outside the chapel, all eyes were turned in the direction of the castle as the cold air was pierced by a blast of trumpets to herald the start of the procession. Just as the first of the carriages was about to move, Henry Vizetelly, a garrulous journalist and publisher, noticed that the magnificent state coachmen were glaring with fury as a red-faced, white-haired man, dressed in plain clothes, marched towards them. The man was treated with deference by soldiers and police, but mocked by a bantering crowd. Close at his heels were two porters, one carrying a common carpet bag, the other a big blue one. With total disregard for the consternation he had caused, he passed through the castle entrance, as though the day belonged to him. In a sense it did, thought Vizetelly, for he was the functionary from the office of the Master of the Household responsible for the Court Circular.

Finally, the great procession moved forward, led by the Life Guards, the sun momentarily glinting off their cuirasses. The first three carriages contained an assortment of German, Danish, Belgian and British equerries, adjutants and gentlemen in attendance. As the fourth carriage drove past, there was a gasp of horror from the crowd, and the ladies shuddered. Two of its occupants, their Serene Highnesses Prince Edward of Saxe-Weimar, a veteran of Inkermann, and the Prince of Leiningen seemed harmless enough, although resplendent in their uniforms. Oriental princes, however, had been popularly regarded as monsters since the Indian mutiny of 1857, and there, in the third carriage, sat just such a prince, turbaned in gold and silver and dressed in satin, smothered from head to foot with priceless pearls, diamonds and emeralds. The Maharajah Duleep Singh was the son of the terrible Ranjit Singh, 'Lion of the Punjab', a convert to Christianity and friend of the Queen and Prince of Wales. The fifth, sixth and seventh carriages were occupied by the representatives of Denmark, Belgium, Hesse-Cassel and Saxe-Coburg-Gotha, who, though brilliantly attired, paled beside the exotic splendour of the Maharajah.

As the numerous processions arrived at the chapel, so gradually the choir began to fill with royalty, nobility, members of the Corps Diplomatique (who were tightly squashed into a temporary gallery on the north side of the altar), Cabinet Ministers and their wives. Old dowagers, living like dusty witches in remote castles, had emerged for the day and now, in their finery, looked like fairy godmothers. From time to time, a gleam of sunlight would stroke gently here and there through the congregation, giving eminence to those it touched. Sometimes the sun shone through coloured glass and lit up the banners of the Knights of the Garter.

Again, by an ironic chance, the Queen's widely understood wish that bright colours should be avoided, and that mauve, lavender or light blue should be worn by the ladies, achieved what all agreed was a beautiful result: a harmony and blending of colour never before seen on any royal occasion.

Below the royal closet, which was hung with purple velvet and gold, two impassive Beefeaters stood guard. Almost opposite, on the south side of the altar, behind the Duke of Holstein and Prince Frederick of Hesse-Cassell, sat Frith dressed in a confection of courtly costume, with sword, silk stockings, ruffled shirt, brocaded waistcoat, a snuff-coloured coat with cut-steel buttons, and a black silk bag without wig. On his lap was a sketch-book.

Earlier, Henry Vizetelly had observed Frith holding court among a bevy of ladies who, he had been convinced, were all desperately coquetting to ensure a place in the picture.

The organ loft, where Vizetelly had a place, must have been crowded and convivial. Apart from Vernon Heath, who sat in the front row with his photographic apparatus, there was a collection of hard-headed journalists, including George Augustus Sala (representing the 'Daily Telegraph') and an extraordinary character, the Reverend J. C. M. Bellew, who was one of the most popular preachers in London and on this occasion was, according to Vizetelly, representing the 'Morning Post'. Throughout the long wait, Bellew regaled his fellow journalists with highly coloured accounts of certain noble members of the congregation. The assembled company in the organ loft was further diverted by the fulminations of James Grant, editor of the 'Morning Advertiser' and a theologian of extreme Calvinistic views. His subject was the sinful conduct of the Corporation of London in permitting Eugene Rimmel, the perfumer, of the Strand, to erect bronze incense-burning trophies on London Bridge on the day that the Prince and Princess entered the metropolis. Grant was quelled only when Sala was able to point out to him his newly arrived compatriot, the Duchess of Inverness, who was wearing a tartan mantle.

All the while, and throughout the ceremony, Vernon Heath's wet plates came clattering incessantly up to the organ loft, to be exposed and sent back again down a specially contrived wooden trough to his assistants in a side chapel below. How hearts must have sunk there as all that emerged from the developer was a succession of plates bearing no image at all, or occasionally a faint blur.

By twelve o'clock, everyone was in position, awaiting the first of the processions from the west door to the choir. On the Haut Pas, or dais, surrounding the altar stood the clergy, headed by the Archbishop of Canterbury. Outside the chapel, in the Gothic hall, the Count of Flanders, brother of the heir to the Belgian throne, was rendering a service beyond the capability of any ordinary court official in successfully martialling a procession composed almost entirely of Danish, German, Belgian and British royalty, some of whom were politically at each other's throats, into some semblance of precedence which would least offend those concerned. By a stroke of genius, the Maharajah Duleep Singh, who was exempt from European conflicts, was placed first, and appeared at the head of the procession when the purple curtains in front of the west door were drawn back precisely at noon.

Their Highnesses, Imperial, Royal or merely Serene, attended by aides, advanced up the aisle and, after bowing to the Queen, took their allotted places. The violet velvet dress and immensely long train of Princess Christian, mother of the bride, impressed the congregation as she swept sedately up the aisle. Duleep Singh, Prince Edward of Saxe-Weimar and the Prince of Leiningen all took their places near the altar on the Haut Pas.

Disraeli recorded how impressed he was at the graceful and imposing way the royal guests bowed to the Queen. He had not seen the stricken woman since the death of her consort and, being near sighted, he decided to use his glass. He saw her well, but unfortunately caught her glance. 'I did not,' he wrote, 'venture to use my glass again.'

To Mary Stanley, Dr (later Dean) Stanley's sister, who had a good position in the south choir gallery, the Queen looked melancholy and at times appeared agitated and restless, moving her hair and rearranging her long streamers, meanwhile asking questions of the Duchess of Sutherland, who sat by her.

At ten past twelve, a flourish on the trumpets followed by a roll of drums announced the approach of the procession of the royal family and the Queen's household. As the fanfare sounded, the Queen could be seen to tremble all over and she could not conceal the working of her face. Wheeling from the sides of the nave, the drummers and trumpeters marched up the aisle to the measured beat of a triumphal march, followed by Pursuivants and Heralds and numerous members of the Queen's household, including Sir Charles Phipps, Keeper of the Privy Purse.

The first royal member to appear was the popular Princess Mary of Cambridge, future mother of Queen Mary, wife of George V. Her curtsy to the Queen was, so Disraeli thought, the most dignified of all. Then came the imposing figure of Princess Mary's mother, the Duchess of Cambridge; behind her were three of the Queen's daughters, the Princesses Beatrice, Louise and Helena. The Princess Alice came next with her husband Prince Louis of Hesse, who was robed as a Knight of the Garter. A murmur of pleasure greeted the Crown Princess of Prussia, 'Vicky', unescorted but leading what the 'Morning Post' was pleased to call 'her sweet little child Prince William'.

Prince William of Prussia, the future Kaiser Wilhelm II, before whom the whole world was to tremble, was then only five and was already something of a handful, who cheerily addressed his grandmother, Queen Victoria, as 'duck'. Prince William was in a fractious mood, although this was not immediately apparent. He loathed the Highland dress into which he had been forced, and the cold wind had stung his small knees on the way to the chapel.

Eighty-five years separated the Prince from one of those who followed him in the procession. The Field-Marshal Viscount Combermere's breast gleamed with medals he had won as a veteran of Flanders in the previous century, of the fall of Tippoo Sahib and of the Peninsula war. Bringing up the rear of the procession were the handsome younger sons of Queen Victoria, the Princes Arthur and Leopold, aged thirteen and ten, and both also dressed in Highland costume. Beethoven's Triumphal

Princess Alice (photographed by Mayall) and her husband, Prince Louis of Hesse.
Right:
Plan of seating in the choir of St George's Chapel from 'The Wedding at Windsor'.

PLAN OF ST. GEORGE'S CHAPEL.

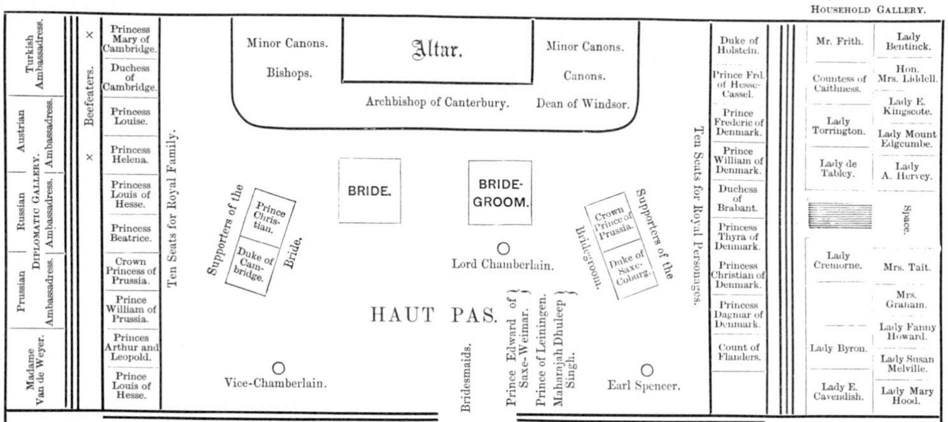

Altar.

Minor Canons. Bishops. Minor Canons. Canons.

Archbishop of Canterbury. Dean of Windsor.

BRIDE. **BRIDE-GROOM.**

Lord Chamberlain.

HAUT PAS.

Supporters of the Bride: Prince Christian. Duke of Cambridge.

Supporters of the Bridegroom: Crown Prince of Prussia. Duke of Saxe-Coburg.

Bridesmaids. Prince Edward of Saxe-Weimar. Prince of Leiningen. Maharajah Dhuleep Singh. Earl Spencer.

Vice-Chamberlain.

Left gallery (top to bottom):

Turkish Ambassadress. — Princess Mary of Cambridge. / Duchess of Cambridge.
Beefeaters.
Austrian Ambassadress. — Princess Louise. / Princess Helena.
Russian Ambassadress. DIPLOMATIC GALLERY. — Princess Louis of Hesse. / Princess Beatrice.
Prussian Ambassadress. — Crown Princess of Prussia. / Prince William of Prussia.
Madame Van de Weyer. — Princes Arthur and Leopold. / Prince Louis of Hesse.

Ten Seats for Royal Family.

Right gallery (Ten Seats for Royal Personages):

Duke of Holstein. / Prince Frdl. of Hesse-Cassel. / Prince Frederic of Denmark. / Prince William of Denmark. / Duchess of Brabant. / Princess Thyra of Denmark. / Princess Christian of Denmark. / Princess Dagmar of Denmark. / Count of Flanders.

Household Gallery (right):

Mr. Frith.	Lady Bentinck.
Countess of Caithness.	Hon. Mrs. Liddell.
Lady Torrington.	Lady E. Kingscote.
Lady de Tabley.	Lady Mount Edgcumbe.
	Lady A. Hervey.
Lady Cremorne.	Space.
	Mrs. Tait.
	Mrs. Graham.
Lady Byron.	Lady Fanny Howard.
	Lady Susan Melville.
Lady E. Cavendish.	Lady Mary Hood.

Left lower block:

The Lord Chancellor.	Mistress of the Robes.	Countess Spencer.	Captain de Falbe.
Countess of Shaftesbury.	Countess Dornberg.	Countess of Gainsborough.	Mons. de Bille.
Earl of Shaftesbury, K.G.	Countess Gleichen.	Marchioness of Ely.	General d'Oxholm.
Duchess of Somerset.	Count Gleichen.	Viscountess Jocelyn.	Countess Reventlow.
Duke of Somerset, K.G.	Duchess of St. Albans.	Duchess of Athole.	Captain Castenschjöld.
Countess of Derby.	Viscount Falkland.	Countess of Desart.	Colonel Clifton.
Duchess of Inverness.	Countess Cowley.	Countess of Macclesfield.	Colonel von Obernitz.
Countess of Clarendon.	Earl Cowley.	Marchioness of Carmarthen.	Captain von Lucadou.
Duke of Devonshire, K.G.	Viscountess Combermere.	Countess de Grey.	Sir H. Bentinck.
Marchioness of Westminster.	Baroness von Schenk.	Lady C. Barrington.	Major Teesdale.
Marquis of Westminster, K.G.	Baroness de Grancy.	Countess of Morton.	General Knollys.
Viscount Palmerston, K.G.	Gentlemen Ushers.		
Viscountess Palmerston.	Hon. Mrs. Campbell.	Countess d'Yve.	Earl of Mount Edgcumbe.
Earl of Clarendon, K.G.	Hon. Lucy Kerr.	Captain Lund.	Mr. C. Wood.
Marquis Camden, K.G.	Hon. V. Wortley.	Captain Kaas.	Mr. Fisher.
Sir C. Wood.	Countess of Caledon.	Colonel du Plat.	Captain de Westerweller.
Lady Mary Wood.	Lady Camoys.	Mons. de Roepstorff.	Sir Charles Phipps.
Duke of Buccleuch, K.G.	Countess of Ducie.	Mons. de Oertzen.	General Seymour.
Duchess of Buccleuch.	Hon. Mrs. West.	Major Burnell.	Sir F. Smith.
Sir George Grey.	Mrs. Knollys.	General Hon. A. Hood.	Garter.
Lady Grey.	Lord Churchill.	Count de Lannoy.	Colonel Vyse.
Lord Stanley of Alderley.	Mrs. Disraeli.	Colonel Oliphant.	Major Elphinstone.
Lady Stanley of Alderley.	Mr. Disraeli.	Colonel F. Seymour.	M. de Nostitz.
Right Hon. William Cowper.	Gentlemen Ushers.		
Hon. Mrs. Wm. Cowper.	Mr. C. Villiers.	Lady Charlotte Denison.	The Speaker.

Heralds. Officers of Yeomen.

Right lower block:

Monsieur Gosch.	Lord Harris.	Lord Steward.	Earl Fitzwilliam, K.G.
Sir E Cust.	Mrs. C. Grey.	Master of the Horse.	Countess Fitzwilliam.
Madame d'Oxholm.	Lady A. Bruce.	Countess of Suffolk.	Earl Russell, K.G.
General Hon. C. Grey.	Mrs. Wellesley.	Earl of Suffolk.	Countess Russell.
Colonel Cavendish.	Mrs. Biddulph.	Countess of Hardwicke.	Duke of Newcastle, K.G.
Colonel Tyrwhitt.	Mr. Aug. Paget.	Earl of Hardwicke.	Viscountess Sydney.
Baron von Wangenheim.	Lord Proby.	Countess M. Danniskiold.	Earl of Harrowby, K.G.
M. de Schleinitz.	Viscount Bury.	Countess A. Danniskiold.	Marchioness of Ailesbury.
Hon. D. de Ros.	Earl of Ducie.	Countess Pourtalès.	
Captain Grey.	Viscount Combermere.	Countess Brühl.	Duke of St. Albans.
Colonel Keppel.	Earl of Bessborough.	Countess Hohenthal.	Earl Granville, K.G.
	Gentlemen Ushers.		Earl of Carlisle, K.G.
Lord A. Hervey.	Captain Purey Cust.	Lady G. Somerset.	Marquis of Normanby, K.G.
Hon. R. Meade.	Colonel Purves.	Lady E. Somerset.	Marchioness of Normanby.
	Count Fürstenstein.	Countess of Bessborough.	Marquis of Abercorn, K.G.
Dr. Becker.	Lady Alfred Paget.	Viscountess Castlerosse.	Marquis of Salisbury, K.G.
Lord A. Paget.	Lady E. Seymour.	Viscountess Bury.	Marchioness of Salisbury.
Hon. M. West.	Lady E. de Ros.	Lady Proby.	Duke of Athole.
Sir Wm. Martins.	Sir A. Clifford.	Chief Justice.	Marchioness of Abercorn.
Colonel Biddulph.	Lord Mayor.	Dean of Christchurch.	Duke of Argyll.
Colonel D. Carleton.	Lady Mayoress.	Master of Trinity.	Duchess of Argyll.
Mr. Buff.	Lord Camoys.	Earl De la Warr.	Sir G. Lewis.
	Lord E. Howard.	Countess De la Warr.	Mrs. Gladstone.
	Gentlemen Ushers.		Mr. Gladstone.
The Sovereign's Stall.	Mr. Milner Gibson.	Mr. Cardwell.	Mrs. Cardwell.

Heralds. Gentlemen at Arms.

DOOR.

THE NAVE.

March (from 'The Ruins of Athens') pealed through the choir as the procession reached the entrance. After obeisance to the Queen, the new arrivals took their seats in the chapel.

At half past twelve, another even more florid blast on the trumpets, followed by a thunderous roll of drums, heralded the Prince of Wales's procession. The royal bridegroom wore the mantle of a Knight of the Garter over the military scarlet of his General's tunic. All traces of a slight nervousness vanished as he approached the choir to the strains of Mendelssohn's Wedding March. The Prince was attended by his brother-in-law, the Crown Prince of Prussia, and his uncle, Duke Ernest II of Saxe-Coburg-Gotha. Few would have failed to note the contrast between the two: the former was handsome (and good); the latter was singularly unattractive (and lecherous). There was a deeply moving moment when the Queen cast her son a look of tender solicitude as he made two deep obeisances. He took his place at the south side of the altar, a little in front of his brother-in-law, his uncle and Duleep Singh.

For several minutes now nothing happened while the congregation awaited the arrival of the bride. There was shuffling, whispering, the rustling of silks and the occasional tuning of an instrument, as the minutes slowly passed. Young Prince William seemed unnaturally quiet; it was not discovered until afterwards that he had occupied himself in prising out the great cairngorm in the dirk lent to him by his Uncle Leopold. He had then hurled it across the chapel floor, where it was lost for ever. Flushed with triumph, he began to fidget. In vain, his mother, stifling her tears, tried to restrain him. Finally, she was compelled to hand him over to the safe keeping of his two young uncles, whose naked knees he promptly bit, and went on biting whenever attempts were made to hold him.

There was general relief when the curtains of the west door parted; but they did so only to emit a group of frightened photographers, festooned with tripods, clamps, boxes and lenses, who had to run the gauntlet of the nave before they could escape to their darkrooms.

All the while, the Prince of Wales looked anxiously at the west door. At last, the trumpets sounded the grandest fanfare of all, and the drums rolled as the bride entered. Princess Alexandra had already captivated the entire British people. To everyone she appeared almost extravagantly beautiful on her wedding day. She was supported by her father, Prince Christian, and the portly Duke of Cambridge. Behind her sailed a fleecy white cloud of crinolined bridesmaids, all unmarried daughters of dukes, marquesses and earls.

As the procession reached the choir, the Queen was already standing; as she leant forward to smile encouragement to her future daughter-in-law, the sun burst forth, shining directly on her white cap and her face, at the same time so nearly dazzling Princess Mary and the Duchess of Cambridge that they had to shield their eyes. On reaching the dais, the bride made a deep curtsy to the Queen and took her place towards

The Wedding Ceremony as shown in 'The Illustrated London News', 21st March 1863. Frith can be seen at the right with his sketch pad.

the north side of the altar, the bridesmaids floating into a white circle around her.

The band and organ, having played Handel's march from 'Joseph and his Brethren', followed with a chorale composed by the late Prince Consort. At this moment, the Queen lost her composure, drew back into the shadows of the royal closet, raised her eyes upwards as though transfixed, then gave way to tears, almost to sobbing. She did not completely recover her composure during the rest of the service. One voice was heard soaring above the others, and Vernon Heath, close to it in the organ loft, was quite taken aback. Jenny Lind, her face bright with pleasure, was singing among the choristers.

As the anthem died away, the Archbishop of Canterbury and the prelates advanced towards the altar railings, and the Primate began the service in a distant though sometimes tremulous voice. But his intonation was clear for the familiar words, 'Dearly beloved, we are gathered together here in the sight of God, and in the face of this congregation, to join together this Man and Woman in holy Matrimony.'

In the tightly packed organ loft, one over-zealous journalist, summoned hurriedly by his editor from the reporters' gallery at the House of Commons, was seen by Sala to be taking the Order of the Solemnization of Matrimony down in shorthand. He seemed quite grateful and not at all abashed when a colleague pointed out that the marriage service could be found, word for word, in a volume entitled 'The Book of Common Prayer'.

The ancient ritual proceeded solemnly. The words of acceptance and promise were almost inaudible. When the Primate asked: 'Who giveth this Woman to be married to this Man', there was a moment of embarrassment: Prince Christian bowed his assent rather than joining the hands of the Bride and Bridegroom, leaving the Archbishop to do so.

When the ring was put on, the pealing bells of Windsor reverberated through the chapel. At the same time, there was a loud booming of cannon, which greatly affected the Queen. To Dr Stanley's sister, Mary, who was watching her closely, the Queen appeared as agitated as if each salvo 'went through her'.

By quarter past twelve, the Archbishop had reached the end of the Exhortation, the solemnity of which was sadly marred by the excruciating sounds of instruments being tuned and by the rustle of clothes as the orchestra rose to prepare for the final chorus. As if caught unawares and impatient to make amends, even the organ began to emit spurts and

Departure of the Bride and Bridegroom from St George's Chapel, engraved by C. P. Nicholls for 'The Wedding at Windsor'.

Royal Family group, photographed by Mayall on the day of the wedding. Left to right: (standing) Princess Alexandra, the Prince of Wales, Princess Alice, Prince Louis of Hesse; (bust) the Prince Consort; (seated) Princess Helena, Queen Victoria, Princess Beatrice, Prince Arthur, the Crown Princess of Prussia. (National Portrait Gallery)

whistles. Vigorous hushing, however, quickly restored order.

Then, raising his voice, the Primate solemnly pronounced the benediction, during which the Queen buried her face in her handkerchief. The Prince and Princess of Wales joined hands and, turning towards her, bowed. A minute later, the Queen retired from view, as band, organ and choir joined in Beethoven's 'Hallelujah Chorus' from 'The Mount of Olives'. In a stream of waving plumes and flaming jewels, the whole pageant swept out of the choir at a far less measured pace than that with which it had entered.

As the guests stepped into waiting carriages outside the chapel, the band of the Grenadier Guards struck up. For the first time in fifteen months, the walls of the castle resounded with military music. Amid a sea of waving handkerchiefs and flags, to strains of music, pealing bells and salvoes of cannon fire, the processions returned to the castle.

After a wedding repast at the castle, the royal couple took their leave, pageantry apart, like any other newly wedded couple. Even the traditional throwing of a shoe was not forgotten, although the Duke of Cambridge, to whom this privilege was entrusted, proved a poor shot as the shoe (which belonged to Princess Louise) caught the bridegroom full in the face. The carriage took the couple to the Windsor Station of the Great Western Railway, where they boarded a train bound for their honeymoon at Osborne House, the royal retreat on the Isle of Wight.

The departure of most of the wedding guests from the castle took place in great chaos. When the last of the processions had finished and the troops lining the route had withdrawn, there was instantly an almost solid jam of carriages and people, with whole families losing touch with each other and their coaches. It had begun to rain, even to hail, and the roads had quickly turned to slush. By a stroke of good fortune, Tom Taylor, editor of 'The Times', encountered the Prime Minister, Palmerston, wandering about carriageless. He rescued the gouty old man and took him to the station, where pandemonium had already broken out.

Mary Stanley lost her party, including her brother, so went alone to the station where she found a dense mob around the entrance. By good chance, she met some friends, Lord and Lady Galway, who entreated her to stay by them for safety. Many of the ladies had been wedding guests and still wore diamond tiaras, which were in danger of being wrenched from their heads.

When at last the doors were opened, there was a stampede for the platform, where it was found that the special train had already departed, leaving large numbers of important guests behind. Mary Stanley and Lady Galway were, together with several others, locked into a waiting-room. Meanwhile Lord Galway was nowhere to be seen. Unable to endure their imprisonment after half an hour, the two ladies managed to clamber through a window on to the platform, where they found hundreds of people waiting for the next train.

The doors of the train, when it eventually arrived, were thrown open by the crowd before it had stopped, and wedding guests and public poured in together. Mary Stanley was unceremoniously hauled, as fifth passenger, into a compartment designed for four.

Meanwhile, Disraeli had been trying to mollify the Austrian ambassador, Count Apponyi, who imagined some slight in the absence of invitations for himself, his wife and all the other ambassadors to the wedding breakfast. When the Count and Countess reached the station, the startled ambassador was borne off, protesting, by the crowd. Disraeli seized the unfortunate man's wife and thrust her into a railway carriage with his own wife and some other great ladies who had lost their husbands. So little room was there to manoeuvre that Disraeli was compelled to sit on his wife's lap all the way to Paddington. When they reached the terminus, there was no sign of any ambassadorial carriage, but Disraeli's was there and Countess Apponyi was given a seat and driven home, to be re-united, at long last, with the now doubly slighted ambassador.

When Tom Taylor finally managed to get a seat on the train, he was not a little amused to see an agitated cluster of 'diamonded duchesses' sitting in third class carriages, some on top of others, with plumes broken and tiaras askew. The less fortunate included the Portuguese Envoy, Count de Lavadrio, who had his diamond star stolen by roughs.

Wedding gifts illustrated in 'The Wedding at Windsor' *Above:* vase in silver parcel-gilt, one of a pair designed by the Prince Consort and made by Hunt & Roskell, 'The Gift of The Queen in the Name of H.R.H. The Prince Consort and The Queen.'

The venerable Archbishop of Canterbury himself had made a determined assault on the crowded station, only to be swept off his feet by the mob. In despair he shouted: 'Policeman, what can I do?'

'Hold on to the next carriage, Your Grace, it's your only chance.'

So he struggled free of the crowd and grabbed the end of the next carriage, where he found, also hanging on for dear life, Lady Cranworth and the novelist Thackeray. Lady Cranworth, baulking at the humiliating prospect of travelling third class, cried out 'Oh, I am so glad to see you, my lord. I felt so ashamed of my place. Now I am satisfied.'

Much later in the day, when Mary Stanley eventually arrived home after battling for two and a half hours through the excited London crowds, again as a fifth passenger in a carriage for four, she was greeted by a despairing Dr Stanley, who had caught the early special train. He told her that even this train had been mobbed, and he had seen the formidable Marchioness of Westminster in all her diamonds – worth half a million pounds – besieged by an unruly crowd. She, Lord and Lady Stanley of Alderley, and many others of a similar rank were only too thankful to be piled on top of one another in the safety of a third class carriage.

In spite of the humiliations and hardships and the inglorious departure of so many of the guests, it was a day that none of them was ever to forget. Indeed, during the next two years, many of them were to be incessantly – and often reluctantly – reminded of their participation, thanks to the Queen's command to Mr. Frith.

Above: one of a pair of vase-shaped candelabra in Sèvres porcelain with ormolu branches, presented by the members of the household of the Prince of Wales. *Right:* jewel casket in gold inlaid with Scottish pebbles, made by Mackay, Cunningham & Co. of Edinburgh and presented by the Ladies of Edinburgh.

AFTER THE WEDDING

During the whole course of the marriage ceremony Frith had made no sketches whatsoever, perhaps to the surprise of his near neighbours, as he occupied one of the best seats in the chapel. Instead, he had made notes of the positions of certain participants.

The service had made a vivid impression on him, and a retentive memory would enable him to prepare a sketch without difficulty. It was also his plan to rely heavily on photography. The first move was made by Sir Charles Phipps, some two or three days after the wedding, in his first letter to Frith since their argument about the copyright. 'It will be desirable,' he wrote, that Frith 'should now get the Photographs or Sketches, or whatever is necessary, of the Royal personages' who were to appear in his picture. Prince and Princess Christian, parents of the bride, were staying at the Palace Hotel, Buckingham Gate, and he was to approach the King of Denmark's Chamberlain, General d'Oxholme, who had been in attendance on the Bride at the wedding. D'Oxholme would doubtless afford him 'every facility'.

It emerged that this gentleman could scarcely offer any facilities at all, and Frith was asked to call on him at noon on Monday the 16th to deliver himself of 'some further explanations' in the matter. As it happened, the only person who could have any explaining to do was D'Oxholme. There simply was not time for the Danish royal family to sit for any picture, let alone be photographed. They were in England only for a very short time, and every day was crowded with engagements.

It is likely that Frith was unable to get his photographs of most of the Danish royal family in their wedding uniforms and dresses taken at all, but that he had to rely on photographs taken on other occasions. It was for this reason alone, Frith later claimed, that their likenesses were consequently 'the worst in all respects in the whole picture'.

The behaviour of Prince William of Denmark (soon to be George I of Greece) was downright churlish. An appointment was made with him at the conservatory at Buckingham Palace for twelve o'clock noon one day, his time being very precious. Frith was to be there with the photographer. After some consideration, the Prince agreed to wear a uniform. When he eventually appeared – nearly five hours late – he was in mufti.

Prince William of Denmark.

A gentle allusion to the absence of the promised uniform was met with a sharp rebuke.

'I cannot dress myself up to please you,' he said.

When a photograph had been taken, the Prince demanded to see it. The photographer hesitated.

'May it please your Royal Highness . . .'

'Show it to me.'

'But, your Royal Highness . . .'

'Will you show it to me.' Reluctantly he was shown the negative and, of course, did not like it. As he turned to go, it was politely suggested that perhaps another could be taken, more than one pose being, in any case, desirable. The Prince marched straight out of the conservatory, having flatly refused to pose again, leaving Frith and the photographer bewildered and disgusted. Nor was that all. But for the kindly intervention of a friend at court in Denmark, Frith would have had to do without the women's dresses and the men's orders, helmets and other accoutrements. As for the ladies themselves, he was not afforded the slightest help; even the Duchess of Brabant, he claimed, was painted from description only. This is not really true: among the surviving photographs used by Frith for the picture is a *carte-de-visite* of the Belgian Duchess facing the opposite way to that in which she eventually appeared in the picture. Frith merely painted her in reverse, altering a few details of dress. Even so, since the Duchess is prominently placed in the left foreground of the picture, this method of working was a lot to ask of any artist.

The Duchess of Brabant.

In the muddle and misunderstanding that attended Frith when he began work on the picture, opportunities to obtain either sittings or photographs were repeatedly missed. What was needed and what was so sadly lacking was someone who could supervise the schedules of sittings, ideally to suit the relatively humble artist first and – an impossibility on the level of protocol – his royal and aristocratic sitters next. To many of these Frith's status as an artist differed little from that of a plumber who had reached the top of his calling. That the one plied his trade with paint and canvas while the other pondered the unmentionable mysteries of drains could be no possible concern of theirs. Frith himself, for all his humour, did not always inspire confidence; to his disadvantage, he often struck those who met him as rather commonplace in both appearance and manner.

However, he quickly won some friends at court. The first was Katherine Bruce, the widow of Major General the Hon. Robert Bruce and sister-in-law to Lady Augusta Bruce; she was also Extra Bedchamber Woman to the Queen. Frith had written to Sir Charles Phipps on 16th March with numerous and very reasonable requests. It was to her that Frith's letter was passed, doubtless with relief, by way of the Queen.

Frith had asked that if the bodies were not forthcoming, perhaps the dresses in which they had been clothed could be sent to his studio. Any female member of his large family would willingly have slipped into them and posed for a heavenly few hours as a princess. But no, as Katherine Bruce informed him, in the third person, in a letter on the next day. Her Majesty, she told Frith, says that she has *never* allowed either her dresses or those of the princesses to be taken out of the palace, that artists who painted pictures of the Coronation, Marriage, Baptism of the Prince of Wales, etc., etc., etc., *always* came to the Palace and sketched them there. The Duchess of Brabant would be at Windsor for a further three days and could 'give Mr Frith a sitting any day he likes to come down.' Princess Christian could not possibly be asked to leave her dress behind her, but, she suggested helpfully, 'Mr Frith might be able to procure some silk of the same colour.'

In a letter two days later, Katherine Bruce told Frith that the conservatory at Buckingham Palace, 'where Her Majesty and the Royal Family have been repeatedly photographed,' would be ready for his photographer on the next Saturday, to photograph the dresses. Either a misunderstanding or a change of mind lost Frith the opportunity of painting the future Queen of the Belgians and her brother-in-law, the Count of Flanders, from sittings, since Katherine Bruce added mistakenly that as they were 'not comprehended in your view of the scene, it will be unnecessary to have sittings from them.'

All the while, Frith had been busy trying to complete a preliminary sketch for his great picture. There was hardly a minute to be lost. Already important sitters were on the move, filling their diaries with engagements or just leaving the country; dresses that were not being cut to ribbons for souvenirs were being consigned to mothballed oblivion. Frith's subjects not only grew older day by day but changed shape and died. Besides, Frith had other commitments of his own.

By early April, the sketch was complete. Frith needed an audience with the Queen to discuss its finer points. As there was only one day, Tuesday, 7th April, available to him between its completion and the commencement of his duties in arranging the pictures for the Royal Academy's Summer Exhibition, he begged to see Her Majesty then.

Frith was granted an audience on the day he had requested and he spent more than half an hour with the Queen at Windsor. During his early audiences with her, all conversation had to be conducted stiffly through a third party: suggestion and nuance were impossible. 'Please tell Mr Frith . . . ' she would say. As this precluded rational conversation and prevented any serious conclusion being reached, the third party was eventually silenced in favour of direct communication. In no time, Queen and artist got on famously; she laughed at his jokes and took an interest in all he told her. Frith deeply regretted not having the comments of the late Prince Consort, whose opinion he valued greatly. He did, however, recognise in the Queen a fellow artist of 'experience and ability', and he admitted to having been assisted by her suggestions. It seemed to him that she was pleased with his sketch and agreed to everything he proposed – even to the length of the picture, ten feet. 'All charming so far,' he noted in his diary.

'So far and no farther,' he wrote over twenty years later. For all too soon his troubles began. One of the first of his many tasks was to write scores of letters, often in a hurried and sometimes barely legible hand, with forms of address a constant hazard. Sometimes his letters were answered, sometimes not. Usually, when there was silence, it was because he had omitted to mention that the picture was being painted for and by command of the Queen. When he did remember to mention this vital fact, consent to sit for his picture was more forthcoming. Among the first to receive letters from him were the bridesmaids.

Frith had lived with his wife and family at 10 Pembridge Villas, Bayswater since the early 1850s. It was a huge family (certainly by today's standards): his wife Isabelle provided him with twelve children, of whom five sons and five daughters were to survive him. The artist was in the habit of making replicas (sometimes more than just one) of his crowded pictures. As in art, so in life. It was as though Frith suffered from a species of double vision which led him inexorably towards the pursuit of a double life. As if one large family were not enough, his paternal instinct was allowed to proliferate eastwards by almost exactly a mile, to Oxford Terrace (now Sussex Gardens), where he was already busy raising a replica family. His mistress Mary Alford had already borne two of his children, Agnes and William Powell, and was eventually to produce four more boys and a girl. In two families, he had a total of nineteen children. Clearly Frith liked crowds. Mrs Frith's suspicions were eventually aroused when her husband had been away for a few days and she saw him in a street near their home casually posting a letter to say that he was having a nice time in Brighton. Isabelle Frith died on 30th January 1880; a year and two days later, Frith married Mary Alford in Paddington.

In 1863, Pembridge Villas was, as now, a wide, curving street. It was approached from London by the Kensington Gravel Pits (now the Bayswater Road), turning right at Albert Terrace and proceeding towards Westbourne Grove, some quarter of a mile south of the Great Western Railway line, which had its terminus at Paddington, only a few hundred yards from Mary Alford's house. Bayswater, which stood then on the very edge of London, was, like St John's Wood, a district much favoured by artists. William Mulready, for instance, had a house at Linden Grove; in the same street lived Thomas Creswick, the landscape painter.

Frith's house was quite new, large, almost palatial, with a grand and elegant drawing-room. His studio, on the other hand, was, in the opinion

of one visitor, the artist Estella Canziani's mother, one of the shabbiest she had ever seen, and all the more reprehensibly so in that it belonged to an R.A., and a rich one at that. 'There was not a thing of beauty in the place, a room not large, very lofty, with papered walls, nothing on them, only over the fireplace an engraving or two.'

It was at this house and in his drawing-room that he received an early caller, as he recalled in his reminiscences. A formidable lady of the aristocracy was eyeing the various ornaments in the room in a state of some bewilderment, if not high dudgeon.

As Frith entered, she turned to him and said:

'I think I have made a mistake; it is the artist Frith I wish to see.'

'Yes,' he replied, 'I am that individual.'

'Oh, really! And this is your – this is where you live?'

'Yes,' replied Frith, 'this is where I live,' and not, he said to himself, 'in the garret where you had evidently been taught that most artists reside.'

'Oh, then I have called in reply to a letter from you asking my daughter . . . who was one of the Princess's bridemaids, to sit for a picture, to tell you it is impossible for her to sit; and as to her dress, which you ask for, she cannot spare it.'

'Indeed,' said Frith, 'I am sorry to hear this,' and informed the indignant lady that he must tell the Queen, who would doubtless allow him to substitute one of his own models, who would have to play the part of the bridesmaid.

His visitor eyed him with an expression which the artist could only interpret as meaning: 'What does this man mean with his Queen, and his model and his independent, impertinent manner?' After a pause, she said:

'Why are you painting this picture? What is it for? Can I see it?'

'If you will walk this way,' said Frith, pointing to his studio, 'I shall be happy to show it to you.'

'What a queer place! Why do you shut up part of your window? Oh, that is the picture! Well, what is it done for?'

'It is done for the Queen.'

'Done for the Queen? Who presents it to the Queen?'

'Nobody – the Queen presents it to herself; at any rate she pays for it.'

'Really?'

'Yes, really.' Then, in tones of respect he could scarcely have felt, he added, 'I am well aware how much young ladies are engaged, and how disagreeable it must be for them to waste time sitting to artists when it can be so much more usefully occupied; so if you will allow me, I will tell Her Majesty, through Lady Augusta Bruce,' that her daughter was unable to sit to him.

Somewhat taken aback the lady returned petulantly:

'Really, I think the Queen, when she asks ladies to be bridesmaids,

WILLIAM POWELL FRITH R.A.:
The Artist in his Studio, signed and dated 1867. (National Portrait Gallery)

Lady Augusta Bruce, photographed in
1860. (Royal Archives, Windsor Castle)

should tell them that they may be called upon to go through the sort
of penance you propose to inflict on my daughter.'

'I thought I had made it clear,' said Frith firmly, 'that I should prefer
to use one of my own models than that your daughter should be
annoyed; and if you find she cannot consent I will write to Lady Augusta
Bruce.' Frith's visitor swept out, saying as she went:

'Well, good morning. I will let you know; I will see what my daughter
says.'

Frith records that the young lady came, and was one of his most
agreeable sitters. By such diplomacy, he managed to lure all except one
of the eight bridesmaids into his grand house and drab little studio.

DOLDRUMS

Frith must have realized, at this early stage, that without a loyal friend at Court he was lost. Here was the commission of a lifetime, but now that he was raised to a position of eminence and responsibility, it seemed, ludicrously, that he might fail the Queen and (a far worse fate for a popular artist) incur public odium. Just as the future looked bleakest, however, there came back into his life a woman who was in every way a paragon and was in close and constant proximity to the Queen.

Lady Augusta Bruce was the fifth daughter of the seventh Earl of Elgin, who is mainly remembered as the man who brought the Parthenon marbles to England. For many years she had been Lady-in-Waiting to Queen Victoria's mother, the Duchess of Kent, on whose death in 1861 she had become Resident Woman of the Bedchamber to the Queen. She was lively, affectionate, wise, strong, and, above all, she bubbled over with fun and humour. After the death of Albert, it was inevitable that the Queen should be drawn closely to this exuberant yet sympathetic woman. As their friendship grew, so Lady Augusta became a confidante and a most dependable go-between.

To Frith, she was faultless beyond compare. She was, he thought, quite 'one of the most delightful women that ever lived.' He was never to forget her kindness to him in all his troubles. One can almost sense the gradual easing of the situation as her influence on events grew. Indeed, it soon became clear that her patience and fortitude were, in equal amounts, prodigious.

Her first letter to the artist was written on 11th April. Skilfully she worked on Frith's ego, correctly sensing that this was one of the mainsprings of his creative impulse and must therefore be vigorously nourished. 'Your beautiful sketch is ready for the Messenger,' she wrote. Mellifluously she sang its praises, appearing to obtain vicarious enjoyment from the pleasure it gave to others, particularly those to whom it was of crucial concern. With great gusts of warmth, she told Frith how delighted Eastlake was with the sketch, how *enthusiastic* he was. 'I cannot say how happy I am to know that you feel assured of the deep interest taken in this great historical work and the earnest desire of all to afford every facility for its completion, and to see it, which it is sure to be, worthy of the Subject and of the name that will sign it.'

Then there were matters of a more practical nature: no, impressions from the photographic plates had not all been taken, so none could be sent before the next week; no, the Dean of Windsor had no objection to him subjecting the altar rail to artistic licence. And Frith was to let her know when he wanted the Garter Robes sent round. She trusted that he would not scruple letting her know 'at any time, should anything further be required.'

Lady Augusta could well have been forgiven had she regretted the concluding words of her letter. For, unknown to her, Frith was behaving like a soul in torment. The Royal Wedding had become a minor industry on a national scale: photographs, real or spurious, cheap prints and souvenirs of every description were being widely advertised in the press and there seemed to be no satisfying the vulgar appetite. Royal and commercial interests seemed at times to be inextricably intertwined to such an extent that it was not always obvious where one ended and the other began.

Among the myriad ventures and projects that appeared were some outline designs published by Winsor and Newton, the colourists, for amateurs of the art of illumination to complete. One was 'God Save the Queen'; another, 'Rule Britannia'. Most popular of all was a heraldic design, comprising the armorial insignia of the royal couple 'with suitable emblems, and accompanied by appropriate inscriptions and mottoes.' Gambart, the dealer, firmly on the bandwagon, was holding an exhibition of photographs of royalty, ranging from *cartes-de-visite* to life-size portraits, at his French Gallery in Pall Mall, the central feature of the exhibition being photographs of the Prince and Princess of Wales. The London Stereoscopic and Photographic Company had stepped early into the field with a pretty illuminated sheet displaying photographic portraits of the Royal couple, embellished with a coat of arms and floral garlands. So much for Frith's imagined copyright of the Royal occasion; it seemed to be dissolving before his eyes.

But the most sinister threat of all came from another quarter, which, most unfortunately for him, was also blessed with royal patronage: this was a proposal issued by Messrs Day and Son, Lithographers to the Queen and Prince of Wales, announcing the publication of two works in chromo-lithography. The first, which was eventually entitled 'The Wedding at Windsor', was to be a full account of the occasion by the celebrated journalist W. H. Russell, illustrated with no less than fifty-six chromolithographs and nine wood engravings.

Day and Son's second announcement must have seemed to Frith like a dagger pointing at his heart. This was the speedy publication of a chromolithograph after G. H. Thomas's *eye-witness* version of the royal wedding, representing the moment at which the Prince leads his young bride from the altar. With undisguised relish, the April issue of 'The Art-Journal' made it known that Thomas was 'by direct command of her

G. H. THOMAS: sketch for Royal
Wedding picture (Royal Collection)

Majesty, afforded all possible facilities on the memorable 10th of March,
and perhaps there is no British painter who can do such a work so well.'

So Thomas was at the wedding ceremony after all. But, unlike Frith,
he figures nowhere in any published list of those present in the choir,
nor is he shown on the very precise plan of the wedding guests published
in Russell's 'The Wedding at Windsor'. Thomas's picture reveals quite
clearly that the artist had visualized it from a point somewhere between
the two sets of stalls on the south side of the choir, close by the upper
tier used by the Knights of the Garter. Russell's plan shows that groups
of Gentlemen Ushers filled the spaces between the two sets of stalls on
either side of the choir. So it is possible that Thomas had been secreted
during the ceremony amongst the Ushers. As she would have been on the

G. H. THOMAS: *Queen Victoria*, sketch for the Wedding Picture. (National Portrait Gallery)

same side as Frith and very likely obscured for much of the time by his resplendent neighbours, it seems quite probable that Frith never even saw him.

But a letter from Day and Son, published in 'The Morning Post' only two days after the wedding, was presumably intended as a counter to any assertions to the contrary and stated clearly that Thomas 'occupied seat no. 1 in the temporary gallery facing her Majesty's pew.' This seat, close by another set of Ushers, is shown as unoccupied in Russell's plan. Wherever the elusive Mr Thomas was during the ceremony, there could be no disputing that he was *there*, and this was mightily perplexing to Frith.

The destruction of the great copyright dream can only have been accelerated by a further aggravation, arising from an astonishing business coup on the part of the artist. If Frith had not taken inordinate pride in the prices he was able to charge, a public disclosure of one such deal might have been acutely embarrassing for him. For on 4th April, a writer in 'The Athenaeum', taking care to remind its readers that Frith was to collect £3,000 from the Queen in return for the picture, disclosed that the dealer Flatow, 'proprietor of *The Railway Station* by the same artist, has purchased the right to engrave the wedding picture for the large sum of £5,000. Such prices,' the writer added, 'are quite sensational – are certainly without example in the artistic world.'

The next issue contained a long paragraph amounting to a protest from Gambart that Frith had been released from the three London scenes contract 'on the verbal assurance, many times repeated by Mr Frith, that he, Mr Gambart, and he only, could and should have the right to engrave "The Wedding Picture".' The paragraph ended with a hint that the case might go to arbitration. In the following issue, on 18th April, was a letter from Frith, who claimed that he offered Gambart 'the refusal of the copyright, and he declined to take it. I then sold it to Mr Flatow . . . Mr Gambart says that I gave him many verbal assurances that the copyright should be his, – but at a price that I thought it worth, leaving him free to refuse to pay the price if he thought it too much. He did refuse; and, very kindly, in a letter written on the day of his refusal, offered to do his best to find me a purchaser, recommending me to an eminent Pall Mall firm in that capacity.' Frith then offered an assurance that he would take up Gambart's original commission as soon as he was free, or refund the initial payments with interest. 'What can I do more? As to arbitration, what is there to arbitrate about?' And there the matter rested.

Flatow's purchase of the 'right to engrave' meant the copyright. If Flatow had paid £5,000 for a property that was disappearing hourly before his very eyes, then Frith's position was invidious indeed.

With Sir Charles Phipps no longer in the firing line, Frith poured out his anguish in a letter to Lady Augusta Bruce, which she received on 13th April. On the next day she wrote back to say that, 'not being competent myself to deal with questions of business,' she had referred his letter to the long-suffering Phipps, 'who shares all our feelings in the matter, – and enclose his answer' (which, perhaps significantly, has not survived).

Frith's distracted state at so crucial a juncture had truly distressed her, she told the artist – not only her, she said, but all concerned; particularly 'in a matter which interests us so keenly and which we had hoped you would have been able to look back on as one of the most pleasurable in your Artistic career and experience.' It distressed her that there should be so much to cause him such 'annoyance and frustration.'

But the good natured Lady Augusta would not let herself be entirely put upon by the querulous effusions of Frith, and she allowed herself a few observations, which may well have reflected the will of the Queen she served so loyally.

'I do not permit myself to enter the subject,' she wrote, 'but I can not refrain from saying that however much chromolithographs and advertisements may attract a certain portion of the Public, I can not believe that this will take away from that large and daily increasing part of it, which has shown itself capable of appreciating and admiring the works of our greatest living artists, and whose interest in such works will certainly not be lessened, should the great National and historical subject chosen have been previously rendered in some different form.'

The message was unmistakable. Frith's sale of the copyright for the gigantic sum of £5,000, even to as astute a dealer as Flatow, was his own look-out. The sale would hardly have passed unnoticed by the Queen, and if Flatow was beginning to regret his side of the bargain, Frith should have thought of all that before.

Small wonder, then, that the painting of the royal wedding picture got off to a hesitant start. Even without any of the mounting difficulties and distractions, composing the kind of picture Frith intended would be a daunting enough challenge to any artist.

Frith's brief precluded any possibility of a generalized conception of the wedding, even if prevailing artistic principles had allowed him this approach. One particular moment had to be transfixed into an eternity, and what better moment than the placing of the ring?

The conception of the composition of the picture was actually very simple. It could be said that there was no composition at all in the accepted sense of the term. The wedding ceremony had been held in a relatively confined space, and, naturally, the bridal couple were to be the focal point. It was part of Frith's design that the guests should be fanned out along slightly irregular radial lines and assembled, here and there, into groups. Here again Frith intended that the great variety of colour should be broken down into harmonic order. In this, he would be able to make deft use of the soft spring sunlight which played over

Archibald Campbell Tait, Bishop of London, photographed by Bingham of Paris.

the congregation and architecture. It was also his plan to put the family nature of the occasion to useful purpose by linking components of the picture through the meeting of glances between guests. While some would look at the bridal couple, others would look at the Queen, who would dominate the proceedings from her position in the extreme top right of the picture. By such means he could invest the picture with a unity which otherwise might have eluded him. A formidable task indeed.

One of the key figures in the composition was that of the portly Duke of Cambridge, the Queen's first cousin, diehard commander-in-chief of the army and a great favourite of the Prince of Wales, who called him 'Uncle George'. In the picture, he was to appear behind and between the heads of the bride and groom. Frith's first application for a sitting was to him and, accordingly, this was arranged for 11 o'clock on Tuesday, 14th April, at his studio in Bayswater.

At this early stage, Frith was doggedly concentrating on tracking down photographs, and by this means he got to know some of his sitters. An early application to the Bishop of London brought Frith into contact with one of the truly great men of his age, Archibald Campbell Tait, who was six years later to become Archbishop of Canterbury. Yes, he told Frith on 10th April, he had a good photograph, taken of him by Mr Walker of Margaret Street, opposite All Saint's Church. He cordially invited Frith and his daughters to Fulham Palace on the following day to see it and to collect the robes he wore at the wedding. Frith probably lost the photograph he was given (that is, if he ever received it), since the one he later used for the picture was taken by Robert Bingham of Paris. A highly cultured man, humorous yet stately, with a taste for literature and the arts, the Bishop must have struck the right chord with Frith, who was to paint an excellent likeness with clear grey eyes and strong features.

Throughout the last two weeks of April, Frith was being continually plied with photographs of the royal family in the uniforms and dresses which they wore on the wedding day. These included one of the little Prince William of Prussia looking bright and pert in Highland costume with his sporran reaching nearly to his ankles, and eventually one of the Duchess of Brabant, future Queen of the Belgians, taken by Ghemar of Brussels.

But how, how was Frith to entice members of the Royal family into his Bayswater studio? During the whirl of the season, their ubiquity was such as to exclude any possibility of a visit to Bayswater, even for a few minutes. By the beginning of the first week in May, the Queen, accompanied by Prince and Princess Louis of Hesse and the younger members of the royal family, had left for Osborne. On Monday, 4th May, Prince Louis drove to Cowes to visit the Princess of Leiningen. On Tuesday, most of the royal family walked or rode in the grounds of Osborne; on Wednesday, they inspected H.M.S. *Victory* at Portsmouth. The same level of activity was followed during the remainder of the week.

The movements of the Prince and Princess of Wales seemed a little more promising, but they were committed to a daunting round of engagements. Frith could at least have made representations at the Royal Academy banquet on Saturday. The Prince had attended to make a speech which had been considered adequate enough, but deficient, perhaps, in references to Art. During the ensuing weeks, the royal couple visited the Royal Academy, the Royal Italian Opera (three times), the House of Commons, the Philharmonic Concert at the Hanover Square Rooms, attended Divine Service at the Chapel Royal and visited the Horticultural Gardens in Kensington, besides giving dinner parties nearly every evening and attending a host of minor engagements during the remainder of the day. Denied any serious responsibilities by the Queen, the Prince, with his young Princess, set about forming a Court of their own. The high spirits and charm of the Prince were already becoming a legend, while Princess Alexandra was learning to become a delightful hostess.

What was Frith to do? The answer, at least to him, was quite simple: if Mohammed would not go to the mountain, the mountain must go to Mohammed. Accordingly, he wrote to Lady Augusta Bruce to ask if he could bring his canvas to Buckingham Palace. He could hardly have caused more consternation if he had gone to the front door and demanded lodgings for the night. She passed Frith's very reasonable request to Colonel Biddulph, Master of the Household, who replied tersely that he did not know that such a permission had *ever* been granted, except, of course, for painting portraits of the royal family (which was precisely Frith's intention). He did not understand how long this picture would take to paint, nor how many people were to be in it, but he did not think it convenient having 'large numbers of strangers' wandering in and out of the palace at will. Even Lady Augusta was at a loss for words and was reduced to making a few non-committal suggestions as she forwarded Biddulph's dismissive note to the despairing artist.

The Prince and Princess of Wales in their wedding clothes.

End of letter from Lady Augusta Bruce to Frith, 15th May 1863.

The Prince and Princess of Hesse
photographed in 1863.

ROYALTY IN BAYSWATER

At long last, on 11th May 1863, Mr Herbert Fisher, Private Secretary to the Prince of Wales, presented 'his compliments to Mr Frith and is desired to inform him that the Prince of Wales will sit to him at his studio tomorrow (Tuesday) at 3.30 for an hour.'

Frith had had to wait exactly two months – which must have seemed an eternity – since the wedding for his first chance of painting the most important figure in his picture. There must have been great excitement in the Frith family at the sudden anticipation of their first royal visit. None of them would have been more excited than Frith's daughters, who were to make a custom of crowding on a red sofa strategically placed at a window to observe royal arrivals and departures.

Frith's hopes, however, were dashed on the day of the sitting, by a short letter from Fisher to say that the Prince of Wales had regretfully been 'prevented by unforeseen interruptions from keeping his appointment' that day. But a letter on the next day fixed an appointment the following Saturday at eleven in the morning for an hour.

This was the start of the innumerable royal sittings at Frith's painting-room in Bayswater. Among the first to arrive was the handsome Prince Louis of Hesse, a great favourite of the Queen and married to her daughter, Princess Alice. But Prince Louis was far from popular in the Frith household. He appears to have been very irritable and impatient, proving an intractable sitter and endlessly smoking cigars, so that the small painting-room was filled with clouds of powerful smelling smoke. All the time he was being painted, his gentleman-in-waiting, Captain Westerweller, stood as stiff as a ramrod. When Frith politely suggested that a seat might be found for him, the Prince barked, as the smoke billowed out, 'He vill schtaand.'

Even without the vaporous prince, smoke in Frith's house was a constant nuisance, at least to his wife. The artist also was an incessant smoker of cigars, a habit he confined mainly to the downstairs rooms. In an attempt to mitigate the noxious odour, Mrs Frith hit upon the device of bustling about the house with a shovel, burning incense bought from a little shop close to a neighbouring Roman Catholic chapel. The addition of incense, which probably did little to ameliorate the stale smell of cigars, sometimes caused dismay in that schism-conscious age.

After the initial promise of his sittings with the Prince of Wales, Frith noticed that there was imminent danger of everything going adrift again. Lady Augusta Bruce had little or no influence as far as the Prince was concerned, so Frith was obliged to turn to Arthur Ellis, who had recently been in attendance on the Prince. Ellis assured Frith in a letter on 23rd May that he had repeatedly reminded the royal couple of their obligations to the artist, but with little success: they had left for Kew three days previously and had not been in London since. He would himself be going to Kew on the following Monday and would again attempt to induce their Royal Highnesses 'to come and sit.'

It was only after Katherine Bruce, now the Princess's Bedchamber Woman, Major Teesdale, an equerry to the Prince, and Ellis himself had combined their powers of persuasion that it was possible to exact a sitting out of Princess Alexandra. Her first session was fixed for 11 o'clock on Friday, 29th May.

Even so, on the day after the appointment had been agreed upon, Frith was warned by Mrs Bruce that the Princess of Wales was 'much occupied now and soon gets tired when sitting for her picture'. She would, in fact, prefer to have two short sittings rather than one long one, and she would consent to sit only for half-an-hour to an hour on Friday and would give another short sitting at eleven on the next Monday.

Her first session with Frith was a most disturbing experience for him. 'That first sitting, can I ever forget?' wrote Frith. To help the Princess brave the ordeal, the Duchess of Cambridge had to hold her hand throughout the sitting. Even so, Frith all too quickly discovered that it had not occurred to her that keeping her face in one position, for a few minutes even, 'was necessary to enable an artist to catch a resemblance of it.' He dared not complain until 'after two or three more fruitless attempts'. With downright failure staring him in the face, he opened his heart to the Prince of Wales, whose advice was simple.

'You should scold her,' he said.

Like his mother, the Prince of Wales was an admirer of John Gibson, the celebrated sculptor – his Tinted Venus (of which the Prince owned a small repetition) had been one of the wonders of the 1862 International Exhibition. Gibson had recently arrived from Rome and with little success was trying to sculpt the Princess's bust at Marlborough House. It was not a good likeness and Frith told Gibson so.

'Well, you see,' said Gibson, 'the Princess is a delightful lady, but she can't sit a bit.'

A few minutes later, they were confronted by the royal couple. To the amusement of Frith who knew that Gibson could hardly contradict himself in his hearing, the Prince said, 'How do *you* find the Princess sits, Mr Gibson?' There was a moment of embarrassment as the three

The Prince and Princess of Wales.

58

looked silently at each other in turn. Finally, Gibson's eyes rested on the Prince; he smiled and shook his head.

'There, you see, you neither sit properly to Mr Gibson nor to Mr Frith.'

'I do – I do,' said the Princess. 'You are two bad men!'

Thereafter, the Princess sat as steadily as the Prince himself invariably did.

Having at last made a start on portraits of the royal couple, Frith's equanimity returned. With a precedent established, he now felt able to approach lesser mortals with vastly increased confidence. The very likenesses of the couple on the canvas not only awakened interest but invited co-operation from hesitant or overbearing sitters.

It is possible to trace the genesis of the marriage picture from these early sittings. Having established the bridal couple as his focal point in a preconceived design, Frith then sought to obtain sittings from those in their immediate vicinity, progressing outwards, engulfing more and more of his *dramatis personae* and fixing them into a composite image. All this could be done only whenever inertia, modesty, indifference, obstinacy, notions of self-importance, sheer fright, public duties or private engagements allowed. Even the medium of oil paint imposed its own conditions: paint needed time to dry between sittings.

The Duke of Cambridge photographed by Maull & Polyblank, London.

The mere act of sitting for one's portrait, too, had its hazards. Frith noted in his memoirs that people 'unaccustomed to sitting, or rather standing – in the fatiguing attitudes required – are attacked by fainting fits so suddenly as to require a constant look-out on the part of the painter for the premonitory symptoms that he knows so well – a deadly pallor overspreads the face, the lips become colourless, and, unless a change of attitude is afforded at once, the model falls to the floor, and work is over for the day.' No-one, apparently, was immune to this mishap – powerful-looking men, soldiers and boxers alike.

Not until 1st June did Frith receive a list of all those present at the wedding. It was sent by the Hon. Spencer Ponsonby, Comptroller, Lord Chamberlain's Department. He also received a seating plan. From where he sat, Frith had noticed the imposing figure of a tall, bald, bewhiskered man dressed in blue and holding a long stick. Standing to the left and behind the Prince of Wales, he occupied an important place in the composition. This was the Lord Chamberlain himself, Lord Sydney, who would no doubt be happy to sit to Frith. The ladies of the Corps Diplomatique, he was told, occupied the front row of seats under the queen's closet. Immediately behind them were the Ambassadors, and beyond these were the rest of the Corps Diplomatique. Lastly, Frith was promised, in a few days time, one of the kneeling stools used by the bridal couple.

Early in June, he obtained a second sitting from the Duke of Cambridge. It was at one of his sittings that the Duke scrutinised the canvas as though looking for someone.

'But I don't see the Duchess,' he exclaimed. 'Oh, she's sitting behind that pillar,' said Frith.

'Oh ah, very proper . . . .alright . . . as long as she's there!'

Frith was evidently to have second thoughts on the matter and, after some delay and not a little difficulty, he eventually managed to squeeze this very large lady in between the dolorously plain Madame Musurus, wife of the Turkish Ambassador, and Princess Mary of Cambridge.

It was inevitable, in view of their prominent role at the ceremony and their subsequent proximity to the royal couple, that Frith should make early representations to the senior clergy. He had already been in touch with the Bishop of London in early April; towards the end of May, he was corresponding with Charles Longley, Archbishop of Canterbury. Without exception, all the bishops delighted Frith. When the Archbishop of Canterbury eventually called for a sitting at 2 o'clock on 6th July, the artist found him in the drawing-room, sniffing the air suspiciously after one of Mrs Frith's incense-burning forays; he said very quietly and with a roguish twinkle on his saintly countenance, 'Have you had Manning here?' It was nearer the mark than he might have thought: the great Roman Catholic prelate had visited Frith more than once and was, his daughter Cissie suspected, of a mind to make a convert of the easy-going, freethinking artist. Like many of the bishops, Longley regaled Frith with amusing anecdotes.

His first appointment with Samuel Wilberforce was probably on Saturday, 3rd June. He was the son of William Wilberforce, the famous philanthropist, and was Bishop of Oxford. No stranger to controversy, he was a genial, jovial and witty man who proved 'a very satisfactory sitter.' He was also Chancellor of the Order of the Garter, and Frith's daughters loved his magnificent robes and blue cloak. Cissie, in particular, adored him and for long cherished a faded photograph of the bishop.

Frith was able to derive a good deal of malicious amusement from the revelation of personal animosities as his canvas slowly filled with people. The Lord Chancellor Westbury, famous for his sharp tongue, had recently crossed swords with the bishop in the House of Lords. Among other epithets, Westbury had used the term 'saponaceous' in connection with the bishop. When the Lord Chancellor sat for Frith, his eye alighted on the portrait of his antagonist.

'Ah! Sam of Oxford,' he said. 'I should have thought it impossible to produce a tolerably agreeable face, and yet preserve any resemblance to the Bishop of Oxford.' And when the bishop saw the portrait of Westbury, he said, 'Like him? yes; but not wicked enough.'

Throughout the months of June and July, the stately procession of bishops came and went; on 8th June, the Bishop of London came again; on 8th July, the Archbishop of Canterbury; on the 9th, the Bishop of Chester. Frith only troubled him twice for his portrait, but

Charles Longley, Archbishop of Canterbury *(above)* and Samuel Wilberforce, Bishop of Oxford *(top right)*, both photographed by Mayall. *Bottom right:* Lord Westbury, the Lord Chancellor, photograph published by Mason & Co, London.

the Bishop sat so patiently that Frith considered his likeness one of the finest of all. He had 'a very characteristic face' and such a long neck that he was known to his fellow bishops as 'Neck-or-nothing brother'. He was followed by the tall, dignified Bishop of Winchester, whose long distinguished career had got off to a lively if inauspicious start when, as a boy at Eton in the first decade of the century, he had written a sensational novel, 'The White Nun; or the Black Bog of Dromore', which he had sold to a local bookseller for £5. The author had been styled 'a young gentleman of Note,' it being plain to everyone, the publisher had hastened to assure him, that 'Note' was 'Eton' spelt backwards.

It seems that during July 1863, Frith was trying to impose some kind of coherence on the unruly group of bridesmaids who swarmed in a white cluster behind the bridal couple. Between sittings, he would hire professional models, use lay figures, or even coax one of his daughters to stand for an hour or two while he sketched in the group. Whenever an opportunity presented itself, he would grasp it and paint a bridesmaid from the life. His stories of these sittings went the rounds of his artistic brethren. At a 'Punch' dinner, the painter's friend, the caricaturist John Leech, delighted the assembled company with an anecdote about Frith's treatment of these 'Swellesses', as he called them. Dewy-eyed and breathless, they would plead with the artist.

'Oh, please be quick with this bother – I was dancing with the Prince till three, and I really can't spare the time. . . '

'Oh, of course,' said Frith, 'I can get a model to do all I want – only if your ladyship would like your face to be *known*, you must submit to sit for me.'

Then the Mamma says, 'My dear, attend to Mr Frith.'

In the left foreground of the picture, almost half way between the Duchess of Brabant and the Royal couple, Frith intended painting a captivating little vignette of the two little princes, Arthur and Leopold, in Highland costume. Arthur, who was to stand on the right, was thirteen years old and was the Queen's favourite son. Leopold, on the left, was only ten and, tragically, a haemophiliac: the slightest accident, slip or bruise could prostrate him for weeks. Even at the wedding, when Prince William of Prussia had attacked his knees, he had been, although unharmed, in grave peril. Frith had excellent photographs of these two, but the Queen owned another, taken by Mayall, of the two boys together; this she might well have lent to him, so closely does it approximate to the finished portraits.

The availability of the two Princes posed as big a problem as any that Frith had. The first appointment made by Major Elphinstone, Prince Arthur's governor, was for 13th June at half past three. Another was made for 15th June. Elphinstone told the Queen in a memorandum on that day that Prince Arthur had remained at Frith's studio that

Prince Arthur photographed by Mayall.

Prince Leopold photographed by Ghemar Frères, Brussels.

Prince Leopold, afterwards Duke of Albany (left) and Prince Arthur, afterwards Duke of Connaught, photographed by Mayall in March 1863. (Royal Archives)

morning 'on his way to Greenwich; and as both the Princes occupy a prominent position in the foreground of the picture, Mr Frith is very anxious that they should favor him soon with one or two sittings.'

All too predictably, matters were to turn out less easily with little Prince Leopold. In his memorandum, Elphinstone alluded with scrupulous delicacy to the question of his sitting to Frith. Prince Leopold could call on Mr Frith on the 17th 'on his way to the Flower show. He could leave Windsor at 9.10 a.m. under the protection of Mr Buff, who had been given full directions and explanations, and as the latter is not acquainted with Mr Frith,' he, Elphinstone, would await the Prince's arrival at Paddington, 'and take the Prince himself to the studio, and there prevent any mistakes.'

Just as Frith's schedule of sittings looked like settling into an unbroken pattern, things began to go wrong. Attempts to induce the Prince and Princess of Wales and Prince Arthur to sit again were unsuccessful. A sitting planned for the Prince of Wales on 6th July had to be cancelled at the last minute, because the Queen of Prussia had suddenly postponed the time of her departure to that morning. The Prince did, however, offer to sit for Frith on the next day. The Princess's round of engagements had become more clogged than ever, and Prince Arthur had to be present at a review of troops at Woolwich on the one day (Monday, 22nd June) that Frith could manage. Furthermore, Elphinstone informed him, the Prince was engaged every day that week. On the Monday after, he had to be present at another review of troops, this time at Aldershot. As for Prince Leopold, the inevitable had occurred: he had sustained an injury – trivial enough, but, as was the way, sufficiently serious 'as to render his confinement to a sofa advisable for at least the next fourteen days.'

In spite of the frustrations, these were busy weeks for Frith. Slowly, he worked outwards from the royal couple, painting a head here and a head there as opportunities arose. In early July, he found time to paint the handsome Dean of Windsor, Gerald Wellesley, into the foreground on the extreme right of the picture; only the Dean and the Archbishop of Canterbury faced the royal couple fully. During the sittings the Dean had asked Frith if he could *actually* sit because of the effects of a recent accident. Later in the month, into a sea of featureless countenances, Frith painted the portrait of Lord Castlerosse, the Vice Chamberlain, whose frequent absences in Ireland prevented him sitting at any other time. Although he was placed well back in the congregation, only three men stood between him and the royal couple. These were Prince Edward of Saxe-Weimar, Prince Frederick William of Prussia and Duke Ernest II of Saxe-Coburg-Gotha.

But there were still well over a hundred further portraits to paint. It was now some five months after the ceremony, and Frith faced the future with a heavy heart.

"UNCLE WALES'S WEDDING"

July was rather a cool and dry month that year. However, Frith was so busy that he would no more have noticed had it been hot and wet. During much of the month he used the time between sittings, as well as the gaps left by the often inexplicable failures to appear, by painting uniforms and dresses. For instance, Prince Leopold, who was travelling about 'in some of the wildest parts of Wales', had lent his Highland costume.

But only too often, there would be yet another frustration, as in the case of the Princess of Wales's wedding dress: thinking that Frith had already painted it, she had had it cut up and altered. But all was not lost, as Mrs Bruce informed him: her 'Dresser promised to send you all she could.' So heavy was the traffic in articles of clothing between the royal palaces and Frith's studio that sooner or later there had to be a mix-up. Like all artists who painted historical pictures, Frith kept in his studio historical props and clothing, even items of fancy dress. On one occasion, he sent an Elizabethan ruff to the Queen, by way of Phipps, thinking perhaps that it belonged to a member of the royal family. Phipps sent the 'absurd fancy ruff' back in disgust, adding that he would not have deigned to bring it to the Queen's attention.

News of Frith's latest frustrations reached the ears of Lady Augusta Bruce, who was on holiday in Scotland. Powerless to intercede on his behalf, she could only tell Frith how miserable she was to hear of the hindrances and vexations which were so besetting him.

Before going on holiday, indeed by the middle of June, Lady Augusta had undertaken for Frith what was to be a daunting assignment: she had written to Brussels asking for the loan of the wedding robes worn by the Duchess of Brabant, future Queen of the Belgians. The Duchess occupied a prominent position in the left foreground of the picture; she was, in fact, in what Frith called 'the eye of the picture'. Not even a single sitting had been obtained from the hoydenish and unpredictable Duchess. The space covered by her magnificent purple robe of moiré antique embroidered with gold was considerable, and Frith could do nothing without it. But Lady Augusta received no reply to her letter.

It was only after Queen Victoria herself had personally interceded

Prince Edward of Saxe-Weimar photographed by C. Silvy, London.

The Count of Flanders photographed by F. R. Window, London.

The Prince of Leiningen photographed by J. Harris, Portsea.

on Lady Augusta's behalf that she was able to procure the robe, and even there the problems did not end. Even Lady Augusta had to admit that it had all been '*very difficult*'. Writing to Frith from Coburg on 15th August, she told him she was 'happy to be able to announce to you a success!' although she had had to make 'promises without end . . . in the most solemn way' in his name.

It seemed that the Duchess of Brabant had had a variety of valuable articles 'rendered totally useless' by 'people of great note' in Belgium, and she had vowed never to lend anything again. Lady Augusta had had to answer for it that Frith never smoked, at least not in his studio, and that it was 'as clean as the dressing-room of the most fastidious lady.' These strictures were followed by various tiresome stipulations. It was only after Lady Augusta's return that Frith discovered the real reason for these conditions, which had been augmented by yet another, that he was forbidden to drink beer in the presence of the robes.

'I kept my word with some difficulty as regards smoking, easily in respect of beer; but why these restrictions?' asked Frith. Lady Augusta explained the mystery: 'The Duchess had lent dresses to Belgian painters, who had returned them not only smelling of tobacco, but beer-stained also.'

During the months of July and early August, Frith was able to paint their Serene Highnesses Prince Edward of Saxe-Weimar and the Prince of Leiningen. Appointments for sittings for Prince Edward, who was Colonel of the Grenadier Guards and Aide-de-Camp to the Queen, were necessarily bedevilled by endless field-days, reviews and parades, but this tall, magnificently bearded man proved a model sitter. So did the rather shorter and less spectacular Prince of Leiningen; like Prince Edward, he proved to be patient, good-natured and tolerant (perhaps even indifferent, it occurred to Frith). Thanks to Prince Edward, an error on the part of Frith was averted – he had wanted to put the Duke of Brabant, heir to the Belgian throne, into the picture. The Prince pointed out that it was not the Duke but his brother, the Count of Flanders, who had been at the wedding.

At the beginning of September, the overtired, overwrought artist, who had toiled incessantly for five months at his prodigious task, took a holiday. It was a shooting holiday and lasted for about ten days. This was, however, scarcely adequate, either as a well-earned rest or to fortify him against the rigours of the autumn.

Frith did not receive the Duchess of Brabant's robes until the middle of September, and even after he had given his solemn pledge to refrain from drinking beer or smoking cigars in their presence, they were to be unpacked and repacked by a professional packer. He was much pre-occupied with the prominent group formed by the Duchess of Brabant, Prince Frederick William of Prussia and the Duke of Saxe-Coburg. The latter in particular was crucial, both pictorially and because he was, for all his depravity, the brother of the late, lamented Prince Consort. Happily for Frith, the facial havoc wrought by bloodshot eyes and a sallow skin was not yet evident. The Duke's uniform was expected to arrive at the same time as the Duchess of Brabant's robes, Lady Augusta told him.

It was about the third week in September that Frith hit upon a plan which would enable him to finish off many of the most important figures on his canvas at one fell swoop. He learned, probably through Lady Augusta, that during much of the late autumn the Queen would be holding Court at Windsor to large numbers of European royalty, and he surmised rightly that the Queen would not be averse at last to his bringing his canvas into their midst. 'Let me know when to propose to the Queen your coming to Windsor for sittings,' she wrote on 23rd September. And on 8th October, she informed Frith that the Crown Prince and Princess of Prussia were going to spend part of November there. 'H.M. has indicated that that time would suit very well for what you propose.'

Frith fixed Monday, 2nd November, as the date on which he would arrive with his ten-foot canvas, and Lady Augusta was able to write to him on 16th October to say that the Queen quite approved of the arrangement. It only remained to find a room to set apart as a studio: 'There is so much less accommodation in the Castle than one would suppose,' and guests were often expected to share rooms. There are guarded references to the Danish princes in her letters at this time. Although they were about to stay at Sandringham, they were proving elusive if not actually evasive. Frith was also worried about the portrait of the Princess of Wales; he had still not had sufficient sittings, and those there were had been less than satisfactory. Lady Augusta took pains, in a letter on 30th October, to assure Frith that she had explained about the figure of the Princess of Wales and that he could expect 'implicit confidence' from the Queen. The Princess was then nearly five months pregnant.

Fortunately for Frith and his picture, the temporarily congested sleeping accommodation meant that he had to set up his easel in one of the state rooms. The Rubens Room was selected as being the most suitable for the purpose, and there, for nearly seven weeks, Frith also held court.

The Rubens Room is high and spacious; on its walls hang several celebrated paintings by Rubens, who had been knighted by Charles I. With indirect access to the King's Dining Room, the Audience Chamber and the State Bedroom, it was nevertheless centrally situated; moreover, it was a general meeting place, and Frith's picture became the conversation piece of the castle, while the painter was able to transfer to the canvas with deft brush strokes the features of any of his subjects who came within range.

G. H. THOMAS: *Lady Augusta Bruce*,
study for his Wedding Picture. (Royal
Collection)

On the morning following his arrival, he was honoured by a visit from the Queen. 'A wet morning,' she wrote in her Journal. 'Soon after breakfast went to look at Mr Frith's picture of Bertie's wedding – After lunch it cleared . . .' Apparently not a word of comment, and this was her first sight of the picture.

According to Lady Augusta, the Queen did not think that she could spare a moment to sit that week 'but would be inclined', she thought, to give him a sitting on Monday the 9th at about one p.m.

Lady Augusta was off on the day after writing to make the appointment. Queen Victoria had strongly disapproved of the motives for her departure. Lady Augusta was being courted by Dr Arthur Stanley, and the Queen disliked courtship, particularly to her daughters and ladies-in-waiting: it removed from her immediate presence those whom she loved and those who served her.

On 6th November, Lady Augusta became engaged to Dr Stanley, and 22nd December was fixed as the wedding day. The Queen was not told until after the day had been announced, and the news was greeted with a storm of indignation: 'My dear Lady Augusta, at 41 . . . has most unnecessarily decided to *marry* (! !) . . . *I* thought she *never* would leave *me* !' However, the Queen was eventually won over to the idea. Conditioned to devotion and service to others, Lady Augusta had found the ideal companion. Dr Stanley, charming and rather ethereal in character, was almost totally helpless in everyday matters. He could hardly even dress himself: his buttons were invariably done up in the wrong buttonholes, he never wore gaiters because of the buttoning they entailed, and his collar and tie were forever coming adrift. Moreover, it was said that he could neither taste nor smell. This particular handicap never ceased to intrigue the young Princess Beatrice who, chancing upon the doctor in a corridor at Windsor, had entreated Mrs Bruce to put a question to him. She was eventually induced to put it herself: 'Is it true that he can neither taste nor smell?' This was followed by an animated conversation on tasting and smelling.

Queen Victoria photographed by Southwell Bros, London.

'Here we are,' Frith wrote to his sister on 8th November, 'cheek by jowl (rather a vulgar expression that) with royalty, and if painting were not so difficult, it would be very delightful indeed; for nothing can exceed the kindness of everybody with whom I come in contact.' He was particularly enchanted by the royal princesses. 'None of their photographs do them justice;' they were just like any happy middle-class family. Princess Beatrice he found 'a most sweet little creature', although a trifle boisterous. Taking Princess Helena's advice, he *overawed* her a little, so that 'she sat right well.' For a while, at least. Then 'she began to take liberties at last,' and Frith was afraid that next time he would 'be troubled to keep her quiet.'

One day Frith was painting Princess Beatrice's dress from the lay figure when the door was thrown open and he was startled to hear a stentorian voice shouting, as if proposing a toast at a public dinner, 'The Crown Prince of Prussia and the Royal Family.' In marched Prince Frederick William of Prussia (who had arrived unexpectedly early at the castle) with his three children, their nurses and all the English princesses and their attendants. At once, the immense room, which could easily contain them all, was filled with the noise of the children shouting and laughing and romping with the princesses.

Frith was talking to Princess Helena, when little Prince William, who had behaved so mischievously at the wedding, came up to him and said 'Mr Fiff'. Like most of the royal family at the time, he was quite incapable of pronouncing his r's. 'Mr Fiff, you are a nice man but your whiskers . . . ' Princess Helena promptly stifled him with her hand. Struggling to get her hand away, he again said 'Your whiskers . . . ', when she stopped him again, blushing and laughing. 'The Royal Imp,' as Frith was to call him, was carried off to the other end of the room and given a lesson in manners, so effectively that Frith never discovered the mystery of his whiskers.

The young Prince, the future Kaiser Wilhelm II, had a withered left arm; he was prone to temperamental behaviour and had thrown a muff belonging to one of his aunts out of the carriage in which he was driving round Windsor with her. He was a continual source of irritation to Frith, plaguing him endlessly. 'As to Prince Willie of Prussia,' Frith told his sister, 'of all the little Turks he is one of the worst; and how I am to get a likeness of him I don't know.' Frith always took pride in what happened next, dining out on the story for nearly fifty years, as Germany grew more powerful and the Kaiser more menacing.

He portioned off one of the lower corners of the picture, which 'Willie,' as his English relatives called him, always referred to as 'Uncle Wales's wedding.' Frith lent him this corner – about a foot square – to paint a picture on. The young Prince was working away quietly on his part of the picture when he was startled by a cry of alarm from his nurse:

'Look at his face! What has he been doing to it?'

Frith looked and saw that he had obviously been wiping his brushes on it, streaking it with vermilion, bright blue and other colours.

'What is to be done? If the Princess should see him she would . . . '

'Oh,' said Frith, 'I can easily remove the paint.'

This he proceeded to do with some vigour, by rubbing the boy's face with turpentine. Prince William erupted into violent screams and struck the artist violently with his fist. The turpentine had found a little spot or scratch on his face. Still screaming, he landed Frith a hefty kick and fled, calling out between shrieks: 'You nasty Mr Fiff!' Taking refuge under a large table, he bellowed and bellowed until he was tired, while the nurse was in a state of some agitation lest he be heard.

Thereafter, Prince William tormented Frith by sitting so badly that he 'failed in producing anything in the picture resembling him.' But they were later reconciled and 'Willy' became fond of the artist. When they

Prince William of Prussia.

met in the Long Walk at Windsor, he would call out, 'Come and wide with me, Mistah Fiff.'

During the second week of November, Frith was granted sittings by the Princesses Helena, Louise and Beatrice, Prince Leopold, the Crown Prince of Prussia and his unruly son. The Crown Prince, Frederick William ('one of the finest and most manly-looking figures I ever saw'), proved an ideal sitter, and Frith did an outline of his luxuriantly moustached head.

How Frith ever adapted himself to life at Windsor is a matter for wonder. Visitors were forever losing themselves, particularly at night, in the murky, labyrinthine corridors and the large, dimly lit state rooms; opening the wrong door was a constant hazard. Even the hardiest statesmen were filled with trepidation should they be asked to dine with the Queen; conversation was stilted and subdued. At the slightest sign of animated exchanges, the Queen would promptly enquire of the subject, and if it were not deemed proper, icy silence would again prevail.

Smoking was the greatest problem. In normal circumstances, Frith was rarely visible without a pall of cigar smoke. But at Windsor smoking (except in a remote billiard room) was strictly forbidden, with notices everywhere to that effect. A favourite method was to lie on one's bedroom floor, head in grate, blowing smoke up the chimney. The Queen had an unerring nose for smoke and could hardly even bring herself to read letters of which the writers had been smoking. After dinner, a long queue would form and guests were conducted to the distant billiard room. So hazardous was the circuitous return journey that a page was detailed to conduct guests to their bedrooms. This was all the more curious as most of the royal family were compulsive smokers.

The Queen finally consented to give Frith his first sitting on 9th November, stressing that she would rather allow him several *short* sittings than a few long ones. Sucking a lozenge before an audience with the Queen was a favourite palliative against the noisome effects of heavy smoking and, before this first sitting, Frith may well have taken this sensible precaution. She sat again on the 11th, the second anniversary of the day 'that dearest Albert went for the last time to London.' She wrote in her Journal: 'Sat to Mr Frith for the wedding picture.' On 14th she again sat to him before going in the afternoon to the Mausoleum where Albert was buried. Frith was pleased with these sittings although they were too short. He considered that, if anything, his likeness of the Queen was probably too faithful and not in the least flattering. Frith's daughter, Cissie, later stood as model for the Queen, the widow's dress absurdly short on her, even though she herself was still at the short dress stage. So small was the Queen's dress that Frith had to resort to an even smaller model.

The Danish royal family completely 'baffled' Frith: most of them would not or could not sit and had to be painted from photographs. To be fair to them, one must add that King Frederick of Denmark had

Frederick William, Crown Prince of Prussia, photographed by F. Jamrath & Sohn, Berlin.

died on 15th November, to be succeeded by Prince Christian, a prominent figure in Frith's picture; and the political turmoil between Denmark and Prussia over the Schleswig-Holstein question was rapidly worsening.

It was all the more remarkable, therefore, that the charming young Prince Frederick of Denmark came to Windsor and was able to give Frith a sitting. Prince Frederick William of Prussia made a point of amusing him as he sat for the picture. For an hour and a half, while Frith painted away, they never ceased talking 'in a language I did not understand.'

As they attempted to leave the room, an awkward problem of precedence arose. For some time, they stood, each refusing to go through the door first. Finally, the delicate situation was resolved by the Crown Prince, who turned about and went backwards through the door, with the Dane, who had suddenly become Crown Prince of Denmark, following face to face. As Frith recalled, probably with less than total accuracy, 'when he next found himself face to face with the Prince of Prussia, it was on the battle-fields of Schleswig-Holstein.'

The Queen's eldest daughter, the Crown Princess of Prussia, sat to Frith on 10th November. While sitting, this highly intelligent and articulate woman tried to explain the intricacies of the dispute between her country and Denmark. But Frith was 'occupied in a painful endeavour to catch a likeness' and was probably, like almost everyone, incapable of understanding it.

As Christmas drew near, Frith finally left for home. His relief was unbounded when he wrote to his sister on 20th December, from Bayswater. 'When I tell you that in less than seven weeks I have finished the Queen and the Prince, nearly done the three English Princesses, advanced the Crown Prince, begun General Grey, Lady Mount-Edgecumbe, the Lord Chamberlain, and some others, and made a most satisfactory study of the Princess of Wales, you will admit that I have made the most of my time.' All the princesses came to say good-bye. Beatrice showed him her wedding present for Lady Augusta, 'a little ring made of forget-me-nots in diamonds, of which she was very proud.' When Frith confided in Princess Helena that he thought the Queen's portrait perhaps a little too faithful and that the public 'would scarcely be satisfied, after the pretty things they had been accustomed to,' her reply, so Frith thought, was characteristic. She said, 'The public – well, you may say to the public that Mamma's children are delighted with it, and beg you never to touch it again; *we* think it perfect . . .'

This contrasted bleakly with the Queen's verdict on the picture she had commissioned. The day before she left to spend Christmas at Osborne, she paid her last visit to Frith, and later wrote in her Journal, 'A year ago that the Mausoleum was consecrated . . . After luncheon, we went to look at Mr Frith's picture, in which the likenesses are not very good.'

Princess Helena photographed by Mayall.

"PUT NOT YOUR TRUST IN PRINCES"

Frith had left Windsor Castle, but his picture still remained there. It was a very severe winter and the royal family delighted in skating on Virginia Water. The days were too short for any serious portrait painting. For 1864, there is no record of any sitting until April, although Frith may well have caught a stray likeness or two if any of his subjects passed his way.

All the same, he must have put in a lot of work in the first few weeks of January, going by train from Paddington to Windsor (a very short journey), because on 29th January the Queen paid Frith and his picture a visit. This time, her enthusiasm was kindled. She wrote in her Journal: 'Mr Frith is here again & the Picture has got on very much & is really a very fine thing.' If she had said half this much to the artist, he would have been greatly encouraged.

With the picture still at Windsor and with scarcely any sittings, Frith would surely not have missed the opportunity to paint in the elaborate architecture of St George's Chapel. The Queen's newly found warmth suggests that Frith's patchwork was at last beginning to look like a picture.

As the days grew longer and warmer, the sittings recommenced. Like spring flowers the bridesmaids began to appear as the season started. Because they occupied a large area at the centre of the picture, they were as important as any crown princess. 'The bridesmaids were kindness itself,' Frith wrote; 'and if any representation of them fails in likeness or otherwise, the fault is not theirs.' One of the first to be painted that season was Lady Victoria Howard, and she was probably followed shortly after by Lady Diana Beauclerk, a great favourite with Frith, who wrote that 'my regard for truth compels me to say that they were not all beautiful, but one left little to be desired in that respect. Lady Diana Beauclerk, daughter of the Duke of St Albans, was not only beautiful, but as agreeable as she was handsome.' She was descended from the natural son of Charles II and Nell Gwynne and prided herself as much on her connection with the former as her likeness to the latter.

Frith worked from a photograph of her taken at his instigation by the firm of Window and Bridge. On 20th May, at 12 o'clock, Lady Diana,

Next four pages:
WILLIAM POWELL FRITH R.A.: *The Marriage of the Prince of Wales* and details from it. (Royal Collection) A key to the painting appears on page 77.

Lady Diana Beauclerk.

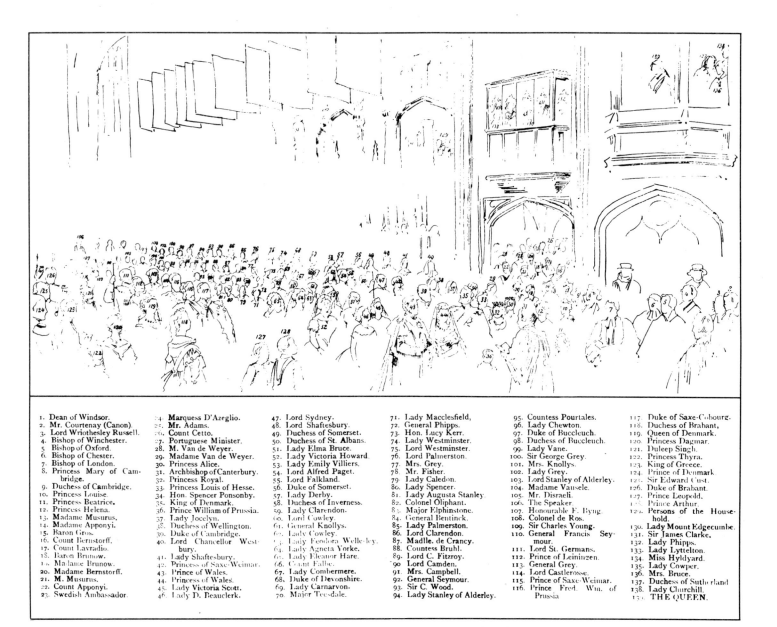

Key to people represented in *The Marriage of the Prince of Wales*. Titles given relate to the time when the picture was exhibited; the King and Queen of Denmark were the Crown Prince and Princess at the time of the wedding. (National Portrait Gallery)

accompanied by her mother, arrived for her first sitting. The bridesmaid, 'a most sweet creature . . . sat divinely for nearly three hours. I made a lovely beginning,' Frith wrote. She had exquisitely golden hair and wore the sweetest of smiles although her pose can hardly have been an easy one, in profile with her head tilted up so that she could not see the artist at work. 'Later in the day,' Frith added, 'came S. Oxon, who stayed twenty minutes to no purpose.'

When Frith later resumed work on the figure of Lady 'Di', his daughter Cissie was sometimes pressed into doing duty for the dress, arms and hands, a task she did not greatly relish.

On the morning of 28th and 29th April Frith received in succession a mild surprise, which may have prompted him to a temporarily more optimistic reappraisal of human nature, and then what was obviously intended as a compliment, but was in reality rather insulting. Having by now acquired a deeply ingrained habit of coping with rebuffs, he would have been startled to receive a letter from the Russian Ambassador, Baron Brunnow, actually offering himself for a sitting (although he had apparently sat before). He even said – and Frith must have rubbed his eyes, for this was so far without precedent – he would be 'glad to hear how the Picture is progressing.' Perhaps the prominence and quality of his finished portrait were not due entirely to the dictates of diplomatic precedence. The second letter was from Major Elphinstone, Governor to Prince Arthur, enclosing 'a couple of photographs' of himself, giving colour guides for his uniform and venturing to suggest to the celebrated artist that the Wedding Picture 'will indeed be valuable, if only in a historical sense, as you have been so careful in getting perfect likenesses.'

So well had Frith progressed with his work that he now began to reach out into the far-flung corners of the picture. He found that some of the figures in the distance were so tiny – Disraeli's head was no larger than a shilling – that he did not need to trouble the 'original', good photographs being 'sufficient guides.' It was still necessary, however, for him to perform a few mopping-up operations in the middle and far distance. With this in mind, and much fortified by having successfully painted most of the royal 'heavyweights', he compiled on 2nd May a blacklist of those persons from whom he could 'neither get photographs nor answers,' namely:

> 'The Duke and Duchess of Somerset
> Lord Stanley of Alderley
> Honble Mrs Willey
> Lady Mary Wood
> Lord Churchill
> General and Mrs Knollys
> Hon. Mrs Campbell
> Sir H. Bentinck.'

This list he sent to Sir Charles Phipps, adding that, without his assistance, 'I fear I shall fail and I can never thank you sufficiently for your kind offer to help me.'

Baron and Baroness Brunnow, both photographed by F. R. Window.

Frith's first appeal to the Duke of Somerset, First Lord of the Admiralty and a Knight of the Garter, who headed the list, had elicited no reply. The second appeal on behalf of the artist, made by Katherine Bruce (who had assumed, temporarily at least, the mantle of her sister-in-law, Lady Augusta), had brought an entirely negative, albeit novel, answer. The Duke, who was celebrated for his very broad-brimmed hat and, as Frith noted, 'a very ordinary – not to say ugly – face,' told Mrs Bruce that he had really no time to sit, but 'could not Mr Frith paint me with my face in my hat, as you often see gentlemen when they arrive in a church – this would involve no trouble and the colour of the robes would look equally pictorial.' The Duke also wrote a short letter to Frith with the same suggestion. 'What do you think of this suggestion?' Mrs Bruce asked Frith, adding, rather sensibly, that 'it would vary the attitude of the Knights of the Garter at any rate!' Somehow, Frith managed to paint both the Duke's portrait and that of the equally elusive Duchess. Of the hat there is no sign.

On 2nd May, Frith made his first application to paint the Duchess of Cambridge, the Queen's aunt and the grandmother of Queen Mary, while at the same time asking her daughter Princess Mary to sit. Ideally, they should be painted together, since Frith's composition envisaged a charming double portrait in the right middle distance. With the Duchess, he had to tread very carefully for, to judge from the photograph which he had of her, she was immensely fat and quite remarkably plain (although her expression was sweet), and she was also in indifferent health.

Augusta, Duchess of Cambridge, photographed by C. Silvy.

The portraits of the Duchess and her daughter occupied Frith intermittently from the second week of May until the last week of August. It all began awkwardly because the sixty-seven year old duchess had worn a low-necked dress for the wedding and her doctor had forbidden her to go out until the weather was warmer. When she was allowed to venture out, the first sitting, a combined one, passed without incident on Friday, 13th May, and Frith quickly succumbed to the charm of both mother and daughter. As a token of respect to Princess Mary, he gave her an oil study of the Princess of Wales. (Her daughter, the future Queen Mary, was to become fond of this sketch and hang it in her boudoir.) Perhaps this gesture was not an entirely disinterested one. We find Frith, on 8th June, only two weeks or so after his generous gift, begging Princess Mary to intercede on his behalf with the Princess of Wales. To finish the bride's portrait, Frith badly needed just one more sitting lasting an hour. Quite apart from Princess Alexandra's timidity in the presence of Frith, she had been pregnant for seven months during the busiest period on the picture, giving birth prematurely to her first child, Prince Albert Victor, in January 1864.

Even the Prince of Wales was proving elusive again. Frith several times applied for sittings during the third week of June, but it was high season and the social round was as heavy as ever. The prince apparently failed to materialise in the studio; several appointments were made, only to be postponed at the last minute. Letters at this time abound in vague hopes and assurances: 'The Prince of Wales . . . hopes to be able to sit' on this day or that, might possibly be able to 'at this hour, no, that hour . . . ' Hardly a day passed without a postponement, sometimes after other more available sitters had been turned away.

Small wonder, then, that Frith was soon enveloped in a mood of blackest depression. Failure again seemed about to stare him in the eyes.

Accordingly, he wrote an anguished letter on 14th June to Captain Arthur Ellis, a member of the Prince of Wales's household. He did so hope, he pleaded, that Princess Mary would 'succeed in persuading the Princess of Wales to give an hour's sitting *one day next week*. I am quite sure from my experience of the gracious kindness of the Princess Mary that it will be no fault of her Royal Highness if she fails, but for the sake of the picture and of my own reputation I hope she may succeed . . . the difficulties an artist has to contend with in these subjects are almost insurmountable.' He begged Ellis to recall his petition to Princess Mary and *above all* to remind the Prince of Wales 'of his promise to accompany the Princess of Wales – any day and *hour*.' Even Mrs Bruce, lacking perhaps the honied persuasiveness of Lady Augusta, could do little to help: the Princess of Wales was, she said, 'so tired'.

There was yet another vexation to disturb Frith's peace of mind. He had lost the race against Thomas, the painter of the rival Wedding Picture. Far less ambitious than Frith's picture, it had taken a shorter time to paint and it was now on view to the public at the German Gallery at 168 New Bond Street (now the southernmost end of Aspreys), the scene of so many of Gambart's triumphant exhibitions. To add insult to injury, it was widely advertised as having been 'painted from actual sittings'. The public flocked to see it, passing through the turnstiles at a shilling a time.

As a solace from the caprices of royalty, Frith busied himself in painting many of the minor portraits and finishing some of the more prominent ones. Among those who sat for him during the long summer months were the Archbishop of Canterbury, the Prince of Leiningen (always punctilious), the Clerk Marshal Lord Alfred Paget (who complained to Frith that he had painted his face too red) and most of the bishops, including the Bishop of Chester, who was eighty and had less than a year to live. His last letter to Frith, dated 14th July, consisted of a long dissertation on street music and ended on a charming note: 'That your hand may long continue to charm the eye as much as Music can the ear, is the sincere wish of yours truly, J. Chester.'

One old gentleman, who lived in Duke Street, St James's, always walked to and from Bayswater for sittings, although he was considerably over eighty and his portrait is one of the remotest in the picture. He was the Hon. Frederick Byng – 'Poodle' Byng, he was called, on account of his once crisp, curly hair. He had been a man of fashion in the early years of the century and had known Beau Brummell, about whom he told many stories. At the wedding, he had been Gentleman Usher. Incredibly, he had also assisted at the marriage of George IV (when Prince of Wales) to Caroline of Brunswick sixty-nine years previously. During the summer of 1864, Frith probably painted in the two beefeaters, one on either side of the magnificent wrought iron gates enclosing the tomb of King Edward IV, below the royal closet. Apart from a few minor details, Frith relied on two photographs taken by Mr Window for his models.

G. H. THOMAS: *The Marriage of the Prince of Wales* (Royal Collection)

Towards the end of June, after weeks of uncertainty and frustration, Frith managed to elicit further sittings from the Prince of Wales, and he even contrived to have his picture set up again at Windsor for a few days at the end of the month. From Marlborough House, Mrs Bruce co-operated with the artist in fixing sittings for the Prince and Princess of Wales and their guests. On Sunday, 26th July, the royal couple spent the day at Windsor and, after luncheon, everyone, including the Queen, went to see the canvas. 'Mr Frith's picture,' the Queen wrote in her Journal, 'has got on very much and is really very fine.'

On the same day, Mrs Bruce confessed to Frith in a letter that she could not 'get the Royalties to promise anything positive' as to sittings, 'but the Prince of Wales thinks he may sit to you at one o'clock tomorrow – Princess Louis [of Hesse] may in the afternoon but I need not remind

Beefeaters photographed by Window & Bridge, London.

you "Put not your trust in Princes" – so do not count upon them. The Queen thinks the picture very much improved and recognised everybody almost – Her Majesty thinks that the figure of the Prince of Wales could be improved upon,' which, of course, had been precisely Frith's paramount aim during the previous weeks. This last observation of the Queen's may well have accounted for the fact that Frith was able to extract the promise of a sitting from the Prince on 15th July.

The Queen's attitude to art was engagingly simple and direct. While she never failed to encourage art in general, she had strong likes and dislikes, quite unswayed by prevailing values; she found G. F. Watts, incomprehensible, Turner *mad*, and later (in common with Frith and, for that matter, almost everyone else) she was to regard the Impressionists as a joke. As for portraiture, its first function was in catching a likeness, and artistic merit was of secondary importance.

Earlier in the week the Queen had been to see Thomas's picture in Bond Street after a visit to an exhibition of Holman Hunt's pictures in Hanover Street. Whatever she thought of Thomas's picture now, it had been clear favourite with her on 23rd March; on that day, she had written to her daughter, the Crown Princess of Prussia, that 'it is as good as poor Mr Frith's is bad.' Perhaps her denigration of Frith's picture was intended as consolation to her daughter, whose own wedding Frith had declined to paint.

Constantine Musurus Bey photographed by F. R. Window.

Madame Musurus photographed by F. R. Window.

Now it was the turn of the Corps Diplomatique, who, with their wives, filled the arch leading to the north choir aisle, below the royal closet. On 13th July, Phipps wrote to the Austrian, French, Russian and Turkish ambassadors, asking them to give Frith every facility for having them photographed in full dress and later, if necessary, to be available for two or three sittings. Again, first off the mark, on 18th July, was the Russian Ambassador, Baron Brunnow, who pronounced himself only too pleased to call on Frith 'on any day and hour' most convenient to him.

The next ambassador to offer himself (three days later) was the envoy for Turkey, Constantine Musurus Bey. He was a very odd character: apparently almost completely useless and effete, he jabbered all day and did nothing. It was said that he did not speak Turkish, his English was execrable and he was probably a Greek anyway. But worst of all, it was thought that he was privately making friends in the City on money matters. His wife was far from ornamental – Frith probably had her in mind when he recalled that the 'aged wife of an ambassador was so shocked by my portrait of her that she implored me to rub it out. She spoke imperfect English, and she said, "Oh, Mister, that is not me. I cannot have grow like that. I will give you my likeness to copy;" and she sent me a drawing done from her when she was a lovely girl of eighteen, with an urgent request that I would correct my libel of her immediately. I declined; and the figure remains a by no means unflattered copy of a very plain old lady.' If this was indeed Madame

Musurus, a comparison between the finished portrait and Frith's photograph of her shows that he did not exaggerate. There was general distress and embarrassment when she died after a fainting fit at a grand ball in London three years later.

From the end of July until the first week or so of August, Frith concentrated on the ambassadors and their wives. Resplendent uniforms allowed him ample scope for dash and colour, particularly with the flamboyant figure of Count Apponyi, the Austrian Ambassador. The Count was most helpful to Frith, and procured a photograph of the French Ambassador, Baron Gros, for him. Seated on the right, the Prussian Ambassador, Count Bernstorff, completed the first row of four ambassadors, together with those representing Austria, Turkey and Russia – a reflection of Britain's diplomatic priorities. Sweden and Italy are sandwiched together behind the front row in the centre, flanked by Portugal and Belgium. (M. van de Weyer, the Belgian Ambassador, for a long time flatly refused to sit.) The French Ambassador is at the extreme right of the second row, and Mr Charles Adams, representing the United States of America (then in the throes of Civil War), stands behind the Marchese Massimo d'Azeglio of Italy. Possibly on account of her size and a certain want of refinement in her countenance, Frith lost Mrs Adams behind a pillar.

It was probably during August that Sir Edward Cust, Master of the Ceremonies and military historian, sat to Frith many times. White haired and moustached, he occupies a position near the extreme left hand edge of the picture. On one occasion, at the end of a summer's day when Frith was much fatigued by his exertions, he said:

'I feel a little tired, Sir Edward; would you mind my smoking a cigar?'

Count and Countess Apponyi photographed by F. R. Window.

Top row, left to right:
The Ambassadors of Sweden (Count Wachtmeister), Prussia (Count von Bernstorff) and Italy (Marchese D'Azeglio).
Below:
The American Ambassador and Mrs Adams.
Photographs by F. R. Window except Prussian Ambassador by L. Haase & Co, Berlin.

84

Sir Edward Cust photographed by Window & Bridge.

'Not in the least,' replied Sir Edward, 'if you don't mind my being sick, which I certainly shall be the moment you begin.'

The closer the relationship of his sitters to the Queen, the higher the rank; the higher the rank, the harder it was to induce them to sit and the greater the expectations of the portrait. This was the cruel pattern which had imposed itself on the artist, and he was powerless to break it. With the Duchess of Cambridge and Princess Mary, charming and cooperative though they were when they consented to sit, he had almost as much trouble as with the royal couple. Again, the dress the Duchess had worn at the wedding no longer existed. No matter; Frith allowed most of her figure to be obliterated by her daughter. Then, as an aid in painting her portrait, Frith was sent a sketch of the Duchess done four years previously by the fashionable artist James Swinton, whose portraits were noted more for their exaggerated sweetness than as good likenesses. What the Duchess would most certainly have regarded as thoughtfulness may have seemed more like effrontery to the artist, who probably ignored the sketch, since he continually pressed her for sittings. On 4th August, Colonel Home Purves, Equerry to the Duke, informed him roundly that there was 'no chance whatever of Her Royal Highness the Duchess being able' to sit for some months, and urged him to make use of the sketch.

But Frith was not to be put down and he persuaded her to agree to a sitting on the 23rd. Instead of his royal sitter he received a note from a lady-in-waiting, Lady Geraldine Somerset, to say that the Duchess, being rather unwell, had taken a '*hot* bath' that morning and 'is afraid in this *very* bad weather to venture out.' Could she see him later in the week, and was she to wear a *low* gown and her 'head *coiffé*'? She was not expected to wear a tiara, was she? Perhaps flowers or a coiffure on the head would do?

During the trying late summer months, Frith painted the Duchess of Wellington and Lady Combermere, the latter after an initial slight misunderstanding. Frith evidently believed that she had expected him to travel up to Combermere Abbey in Cheshire with his picture to paint her head and shoulders – no larger than a halfpenny – into the picture. Frith disabused her on this point, only to be told tartly that 'Of course Lady Combermere never could have thought that he would bring a painting as large as the house into Cheshire – but fancied that he might sketch his heads and then copy them into the painting.' Field-Marshal Lord Combermere, aged ninety-one, died before the picture was finished and is therefore not represented.

Without doubt, the most exotic touch in the Wedding Picture is the portrait of the Maharajah Duleep Singh. Proudly and conspicuously he stands, a symbol of Empire, a most demonstrative token of the Queen's Majesty and no less eminent than the Koh-i-noor diamond that had been surrendered to her upon the annexation of the Punjab, of which Duleep Singh himself had been the last ruler.

In 1864, he was only twenty-six, a Christian, almost an English country gentleman, a keen shot and an amateur photographer. His elderly and scheming mother had quite recently died in her house in Kensington. Here her neighbours had been scandalized, it was said, by the sight of animals for household consumption being killed in the garden, which was patrolled by strangely accoutred falconers, hawk on wrist.

Frith had been in pursuit of the Indian Prince since July of the previous year, always without success, but with a few near misses. Both he and Colonel Oliphant, who had been pressed into the service of the reluctant Maharajah as an equerry, were mentioned in the letter which accompanied the black list that the artist had sent to Phipps. To Frith's disgust, they had both left in January for a long visit to Bombay. When they returned in September, Frith pounced. 'I have written to the Maharajah to ask for sittings,' he told Phipps on 9th October, 'but I fear without your help I shall have great difficulty. Could you say a word for me? The picture is now approaching finish, though it will be some three or four months yet, I fear, before it receives the final touches – the Maharajah is very prominent and it will be a very serious drawback indeed to the picure, if he refuses to sit or to lend his dress, etc.' At his country seat, Elveden, the Maharajah received a stern rebuke from Phipps, who wrote to Frith on 13th October to say that he now had no doubt that the prince would give him 'every facility'.

Maharajah Duleep Singh and his wife, both photographed by A. Claudet, London.

After some prevarication, Duleep Singh eventually sat to Frith that autumn. His eastern apparel must have afforded the artist a welcome contrast from the relative monotony of European uniforms, however dashing. He was covered with jewels. They hardly blazed, Frith thought, the diamonds being uncut and looking to him for all the world like 'bits of dull glass'. So fabulously valuable were they, however, that the Maharajah would allow them to remain at Frith's house only on condition that his servant stayed with them by day; at night they were to be deposited at Coutts's bank. 'This the servant promised,' wrote Frith, 'but, seeing that I possessed a burglar-proof iron safe, he trusted them to its keeping, and me with the keys, remarking: "Now, if the Prince knew of this, he would be awake all night."'

The artist possessed an excellent photograph of the Maharajah which, but for the position of the arms, closely resembles the finished portrait. To Frith, Duleep Singh's face was handsome 'but somewhat expressionless'. As he carefully painted the Indian's likeness on the canvas, Frith considered the man before him: it seemed strange to him to be painting the portrait of the man born to rule a country far larger than England and who now found himself, jewels and all, assisting at the wedding of a barbarian on a little island and compelled to sit for his likeness and to allow his jewels to be copied by one whose neck, under other circumstances, it might have been his delight to wring. But he took comfort from the Maharajah's servant, who had assured him that the Bible was the only book he ever read; he knew it from cover to cover.

TRIUMPH & AFTERMATH

Callers at the painting room at 7 Pembridge Villas in November 1864 would have noticed that the Wedding Picture was very nearly finished. Perhaps to the lay observer it looked completely finished, but Frith was a conscientious man and, knowing every square millimetre of the picture, he was all too well aware that there were still months of intermittent work ahead.

On 17th November, he was able to tell Phipps that 'the time has at last arrived when I shall find the *frame* for my picture very useful to me in finishing and I write to ask if I may order it from my own frame-maker, of any pattern that I think suitable to the picture – or if Her Majesty has any commands to give me on the subject.' The Queen, Phipps informed him on the next day, left the choice entirely to him.

For nearly two months, Frith was left to his own devices, with scarcely a sitter crossing his threshold, Duleep Singh being a rare and tardy exception. His only communications from the royal household during the dark winter months were a letter from Mrs Bruce on 10th January offering to bring him the cross she had worn round her neck at the wedding and another on 21st January acknowledging its receipt from Frith. She was one of three ladies who shared the royal closet with the Queen.

The picture was intended for the Summer Exhibition at the Royal Academy that year, but, before submitting it, Frith very rightly deemed it fitting that the Queen, to whom, after all, the picture belonged, should see it in its all but finished state. The Queen often paid visits to artists in their studios, and now it was to be the turn of Frith, who had not been thus honoured before. 'I am to ask how it is with your picture,' Lady Augusta Stanley wrote on 10th March; she was still in attendance on the Queen. 'Is it visible and how long will it remain so?' It was left only to fix the date.

Frith was given ample warning of the impending visit, which was arranged for 28th March. He submitted the picture to the Royal Academy and obtained permission from the President and Council to retain the picture for finishing. On 27th March, Frith received a telegram which read: 'Be prepared for a royal visit to your studio tomorrow between twelve and one o'clock.'

On the next day, the Queen left Windsor for Paddington at twenty minutes to twelve by special train. It was 'a fine bright morning & warmer,' she noted in her Journal. She was accompanied by King Leopold I of the Belgians, the Princesses Helena and Louise, and a suite consisting of the Countess of Gainsborough, Lady Augusta Stanley and equerries. It was a tight schedule: two other artists' studies were to be visited, and she was due to hold Court at Buckingham Palace at a quarter past one. Prince Alfred, then aged twenty-one, had left for London by an earlier train.

There was, of course, high excitement in the Frith household; the artist's children had taken up their positions on the red sofa in the window long before the Queen was due. As they waited, with growing impatience, a mounted gentleman or groom rode up to the house, announcing that 'The Queen will be here in half-an-hour.' He was followed by another who said, 'The Queen will be here in twenty minutes.' A third said, 'The Queen will be here in ten minutes;' then the last, 'The Queen is in sight.'

When she arrived, she could not have known (whether she would have been amused to know is another matter) that the 'pretty, smart parlour-maid in orthodox cap, apron and black dress, who opened the gate to her' was Frith's sister, curiously enough her namesake and born on her birthday. Vicky, as she was known, had begged to play this role, so as to see closely the woman 'her loyal heart adored'. Frith himself stood at the foot of the steps, bowing profoundly, until the Queen shook him by the hand. His daughter, Cissie, who recorded her memories of this visit many years later, thought that it was in the drawing-room that Frith's wife, Isabelle, was introduced to the Queen. She remembered a young member of the royal party saying in a very loud voice, 'I didn't know artists lived in such big houses,' only to be reduced to instant silence by a withering look from the Queen.

As the party was conducted to the studio, the Friths must have been not only surprised that King Leopold should be there but also startled at his appearance. At the age of seventy-five, in the last year of his life, he was clean shaven, with ghastly sunken cheeks which were brightly rouged, and his eyebrows were darkly pencilled. Always to be seen in an absurdly anachronistic wig, brushed forward in the Regency manner, he had recently acquired a new one, with a dandified curl in the centre of his forehead.

As they looked at 'Bertie's wedding picture' Frith could only be aware of its shortcomings, and even more aware that they would not escape the Queen, but 'she found little or no fault,' he wrote, 'and left me under the impression that I had succeeded as well as could be expected, considering the great difficulties of the task.'

Short though her visit was, the minutes dragged for those on the red sofa. First the children wondered how she liked the picture; then 'if she had turned Papa into a Lord, which we much feared she would do; then

Lady Augusta Stanley *née* Bruce *(above)* ;
the Belgian Ambassador and Mme Van
de Weyer, both photographed by F. R.
Window.

if she were making him paint the picture out and was standing over him while he did it over again.' But they had not long to wait, and the Queen departed with the same ceremony as she had arrived. As soon as Vicky had closed the gate on the retreating carriage, she went into peals of delighted laughter at her own impersonation of a parlour-maid. As the children rushed excitedly to their father, Frith danced a fandango at the foot of the steps. Breathlessly they fired questions at him.

'Well, what did she say?'

'Did she like it? And are you a Lord?'

The eight-year-old Princess Beatrice liked it, said Frith, 'and that's enough for you.'

There is no disguising the disappointment in Cissie's memoirs that her father had only received the Queen's thanks, 'yes, her thanks, though neither then nor at any other time was she ever moved to make him anything approaching a Lord.' Was Cissie, perhaps, endorsing Frith's sentiments when she wrote that the Crown Princess of Prussia 'was the simplest, sweetest, and the most really artistic member of the royal family. She knew about and cared for art'? What artist had the Prince of Wales, when he became Edward VII 'honoured, or asked to his table as he invites actors and rich financiers? Not one, that I personally could name.' Cissie more than once proclaimed that all the Frith family were republicans at heart, and one wonders how much of this can be ascribed to Frith's tribulations while painting the Wedding Picture.

From the time of the Queen's visit until shortly before the Private View on 28th April, it was a race against the clock. During these few last precious weeks, Frith finished off the good and kindly Lady Augusta Stanley, whose tiny portrait was only a few inches away from the Duke of Saxe-Coburg, and the Belgian Ambassador, van de Weyer, and his wife, who were only finally persuaded to sit by Sir Edward Cust who convinced them of 'the immortality it would confer upon them.' Even at this late stage, there was a snag, this time from the second Duke and Duchess of Wellington; the Duke had refused to lend the Duchess's diamonds, since he was prevented from doing so by an Act of Parliament, but he offered Frith a photograph of the jewels. The diamonds later were admitted to Frith's painting room, but only on the person of the duchess, whose portrait the artist had apparently already completed.

The Marriage of the Prince of Wales (together with two smaller paintings) was the first picture that Frith had exhibited at the Royal Academy for two years; it was a sensation. It hung in the East Room of the Royal Academy's old quarters, which were shared with the National Gallery in Trafalgar Square. From the Private View onwards, the crowds pressed forward eagerly to scrutinize every inch of it. Every expression of pleasure testified to the delight of recognition, as the great room was filled with excited whisperings and murmurs of approval. It was, after all, a breath-taking spectacle. As Frith well knew, the British public in Victorian times enjoyed being made to part company with its breath.

On Monday 2nd May, the day the public were admitted, it became abundantly clear from the start that the success of *Ramsgate Sands* and *The Derby Day* was about to be repeated. Two policemen were needed to keep the milling throng at a proper distance from the picture. Success was doubly assured when it was agreed – 'after a fight' – to place an iron rail in front of it.

The picture was extensively reviewed, indeed was singled out for special treatment throughout the press. The reviews were, as usual, mixed – a predictable fact, which afforded Frith considerable amusement, all the more so as he never bothered to read them, good, bad or indifferent, considering that the sale of the picture was the artist's only true concern.

'The Art-Journal', making amends for its early attacks, saw 'the ceremony and the picture which records it [as] a living and a lasting chronicle of England's power, wealth and greatness,' and dwelt at length on the delicately modulated colour harmonies, 'the whites, for instance, of varying hue – the pearly white, which passes into yellow, the shadowed white in half eclipse, and the white which reflects the full shower of light.' Like most of the critics, the reviewer noted the special difficulties such a subject presented and the artist's triumph over these limitations.

The 'Morning Post' noted, similarly, that 'in the depicting of such ceremonies, it is the executive, not the imaginative powers of the artist that are called into play,' and proceeded to congratulate the artist on his virtuosity in this respect, dwelling again on the beautifully maintained balance of colour and the deployment of the groups of participants. Some reviewers indulged in recognition exercises and it would have amused Frith to note how frequently Disraeli, painted from a photograph, was recognised. Many a sour note was struck, however. A reviewer in the 'Daily Telegraph', for instance, detected 'inharmonious patches of crimson, purple and gold' which jarred 'upon the eye'; the picture was *airless*, and abounded in tricks; above all, it lacked refinement – 'we miss the lady and the gentleman.' But, he conceded, 'on the endless difficulties which beset the unfortunate man, who is called on to do justice thus to half the Court, one need not dwell – they will be patent enough to any one who has witnessed the whims of a single sitter; and, however often he may have called in and blessed the photograph, Mr Frith must have had fifty sitters.' The 'Spectator' reviewer was far more dismissive, professing to find it difficult to see 'any interest in the work beyond the sort of interest which every true Briton must necessarily feel in looking at the portraits of so many eminent "swells".'

With the acclaim still ringing in his ears, Frith, ever pragmatic, put pen to paper. There was just one little matter that seemed likely to be overlooked in the general excitement. Accordingly, on 2nd May, the day

Top row, left to right:
Lord and Lady Palmerston, the Marquess of Westminster.
Bottom row:
Lord Shaftesbury, Lady Charlotte Denison, John Evelyn Denison (Speaker of the House of Commons).
Lord Palmerston by Window & Bridge, The Speaker by Caldesi Blanford & Co. Others by F. R. Window.

after the exhibition had opened to the public, he wrote to Phipps. After informing him that it had been found necessary to station two policemen by the picture, then place a rail in front, he went on to weightier matters.

'As the picture is now completely finished, I hope I shall not be thought unreasonable if I ask for payment for it; I am told this is the proper thing for me to do, and indeed it has taken me so long – exactly twice as long as I expected – and has been in other ways a very expensive work, so that the money is very much needed.'

Now Frith raised a hoary old ghost which had haunted him ever since his early arguments with Phipps, and, as the latter made no mention of the subject in his reply, it may be fairly said that Frith had the last word.

'I may mention,' he continued, 'that the copyright was so seriously damaged by Mr Thomas's picture that I felt bound to return a large portion of the copyright money [to Flatow], so that my application – even if it were unused – might be excused.

'I think I may say that the picture seems completely successful with the artists and the public, but I am well aware how far it falls short of what it should be. Still I have done my best, and it would be a great satisfaction to me to know that Her Majesty is satisfied with the result of my work.'

With characteristic brevity, Sir Charles replied in a letter of 5th May:

'I have much pleasure in enclosing you a cheque for the price of your great work, and congratulating you upon the completion of it.

'I think it looks remarkably well at the Exhibition. I believe that a more difficult task never was undertaken by any man.

'I did not fail to speak to Sir Charles Eastlake upon the evening of the Royal Academy dinner, and he promised me that a railing should be placed in front of the picture to guard it from possible danger.'

So Frith's great ordeal was all but over. Like many an ordeal, it was one that enriched his life. He could already number among his friends and acquaintances, many artists and men of letters, particularly Dickens. Now he could add to this select company many of the peers, both temporal and spiritual, as well as many of the grandest and most powerful sovereigns in the world, and others who were to become kings, queens and emperors, whose own particular destinies were to shape the history of the world. As he grew older – and he had over forty years to live – so his mind would travel back to the glittering procession of celebrities who had sat for his picture. When he died in 1909, most of those who had sat to him were already dead.

Casual and carefree in so many matters, he put all the photographs he had used for the picture into an album, and, wherever possible, got his princely sitters to sign, often with elaborate flourishes, as befitted their station. Little Princess Beatrice cried out, after carefully writing her name, 'Oh! Stop, Mr Frith. I've forgotten my flourish.' (Queen Mary was lent this album for some time to check the names and identify the photographs.) He was also very proud of a book in which all royalty

Top row, left to right:
The Duchess of St Albans (photographed by F. R. Window), Sir Charles and Lady Caroline Grey (Jabez Hughes, Ryde, Isle of Wight), Viscount Falkland (F. R. Window).
Bottom row:
Hon. C. Villiers (Window & Bridge), Prince Alfred, afterwards Duke of Edinburgh (Moffat, Edinburgh), Lord Derby (A. Marion, London). More *cartes-de-visite* from Frith's album.

visiting his house had signed their names. On the occasion of a Private View at his house, he displayed the book on a table in his drawing-room, where it was stolen from under his nose. In spite of the most exhaustive efforts, he never managed to recover it. In 1878, his son Walter collected and arranged all the letters relating to the Wedding Picture and pasted them in a large album, but with little regard to chronology.

The picture hangs at Windsor Castle today, not far from Thomas's picture, and there is a smaller replica of Frith's work at the Walker Art Gallery, Liverpool. To some extent, Frith's great picture at Windsor disarms criticism; it is so very patently the representation of a great state occasion painted to order. But one can admire it nonetheless for its coherence as a composition, for the handling of the paint, particularly in the architectural details of the chapel, while even the tiniest countenance proclaims itself a portrait. Close inspection tends to incline one to a belief that some of the portraits are better than others; but perhaps this is, in any case, inevitable. Whether or not considered as portraits, some figures are painted with far more vigour than others and – most crucially – none more so than the central face and figure of Prince Christian of Denmark, who, in close proximity, seems to overshadow the bridal pair. His strong features are all too favourably in contrast with the sensitive, rather hesitant pose of the Prince of Wales who, translated into pictorial terms, somehow fails to dominate at his own wedding – the fate of many a bridegroom. Seen in this light, the Queen's vacillations over the success of the work she had commissioned are readily understandable.

What was the effect, if any, on Frith of his two year ordeal? It is hard to escape the conclusion that the experience dealt his artistic career a mortal blow. He never really recovered the old zest he had displayed in *Ramsgate Sands*, *The Derby Day* and *The Railway Station*. Although, as a work of art (if such it is), it cannot be judged by the same criteria as these pictures, *The Marriage of the Prince of Wales* represents the zenith of this particular genre; its sheer size, scale, complexity and the anguish with which it was painted set it apart from the others. In Frith's career it stands like an epitaph.

Walter Sickert was clearly of this opinion. An artist of stature, he was also an acute professional art critic; in 'The Burlington Magazine' of December 1922, he expressed great admiration for *The Derby Day*, and, perhaps unaware of the less accessible Wedding Picture that followed it, went on: 'the tragic element in the career of Frith is that the immense effort of such a monument as *The Derby Day* must have gone far to account for the premature exhaustion of his talent.' Sickert had hit on the truth, but the truth about the wrong picture. It was *The Marriage of the Prince of Wales* that did for Frith.

Although Frith argues very clearly to the contrary in his reminiscences, it was as if, during the aftermath, he could hardly face the reality of the world about him and he relapsed into painting scenes from history and historical imagination. He could hire his own professional models and call the tune. 'I should have preferred,' he wrote, 'to have carried out my agreement with Mr Gambart for the *Streets of London* and much regret now that I did not do so. I fancied that gentleman had grown cool on the subject of the *Streets*; and when I showed him the sketch for *Charles II's Last Sunday*, he expressed himself so warmly in favour of it in preference to the *Streets* that I accepted a commission from him for three thousand guineas, and at the same time consented to cancel our agreement for the extensive and expensive subjects of the *London Streets* . . . Those pictures are, and ever will be, in the air – a matter of everlasting regret to me, from my conviction that my reputation will rest on the pictures I have painted from the life about me.'

No blame for this situation can be attached to Queen Victoria. As she had a very understandable desire that her son's wedding should be commemorated in a manner that fitted the event, she could be expected to turn to the artist who had most ably demonstrated his qualifications for the commission. Blame can more justly be levelled in a rather less easily defined direction: towards the whole apparatus of monarchy as it existed in the 1860s, its relationship to art, and its responsibilities towards artists.

There were to be momentary flickers of Frith's old self, the same mastery of technique displayed, in such pictures as *The Salon d'Or, Homburg* of 1871, *The Road to Ruin* series of 1878, and *The Private View* of 1881, but in the last picture a rather too fashionable deference to the brown tones of Orchardson and a certain dryness in the handling show only too clearly that Frith had lost his old mastery – if he had ever really recovered it. Whereas in the Wedding Picture it is possible to admire the handling of paint amid all the notabilities, in *The Private View* only the plenitude of celebrities and their careful grouping beguile the onlooker. The artistry of *The Derby Day* had capitulated before the mechanics of reportage.

As he grew older, Frith fell back on repetition, the repetition of old themes under a new guise, the painting of replicas. As Cissie wrote, most movingly, 'while his enormous family was growing up, and when his powers failed, he yet sold replicas of all his well-known works, and always had the Academy pension as a stay! How he managed to sell those copies I do not know, neither can I understand how he could have gone over line for line the pictures he painted when life was radiantly happy and all was bliss and comfort for us all. I should have imagined his heart would have broken under the task, that it did not accounts for many things I for one have never been able to understand in his life.'

Frith paid dearly for the completion of a task he would gladly have avoided, but no loyal subject could have refused his sovereign twice. There is a certain grand solemnity in Phipps's verdict: 'I believe that a more difficult task never was undertaken by any man.' He knew.

ACKNOWLEDGEMENTS

My first thanks are due to Her Majesty the Queen for graciously allowing me access to the documents in the Royal Archives at Windsor Castle which relate to Frith's Royal Marriage picture. This has enabled me to quote freely from unpublished entries in Queen Victoria's Journal and other manuscript sources. I am deeply indebted, too, to Diana, Lady Thomas for her generosity in allowing me to retain for a long time the voluminous collection of unpublished letters relating to Frith's Royal Marriage picture, of which I have been able to make the fullest use. My gratitude to her extends also to the loan of the album of *cartes-de-visite* most of which are illustrated in this book. I must acknowledge with thanks the help given to me by Sir Robin Mackworth-Young, K.C.V.O., Librarian of Windsor Castle, for kindly putting material at my disposal. Lady Millar most generously sought out relevant documents and brought these to my attention, and to her I owe my thanks; these are also due to Miss Jane Langton, M.V.O. and Miss Frances Dimond, Registrar and Assistant Registrar of the Royal Archives.

Sir Oliver Millar, K.C.V.O., F.S.A., Surveyor of The Queen's Pictures, kindly read the typescript and made useful suggestions, as did Mr Nicolas Barker and Mr Henry Ford; the latter also read and helped to correct the proofs. To all these I am profoundly grateful. Any mistakes which may yet appear are, nevertheless, my own. Among others I must thank are Miss Bridget Lakin for help with genealogical research, Miss Sophia Ryde who typed my transcripts of the Frith papers and my niece, Miss Venetia Maas for typing the manuscript, and the staff of the London Library. Lastly, thanks are due to my wife whose ever watchful eye averted many a lapse during the writing of this account.

Sources of illustrations are indicated, where relevant, in the captions. Pictures from the Royal Archives and the Royal Collection are reproduced by gracious permission of Her Majesty the Queen.

REFERENCES

The Royal Archives, Windsor Castle.

Victorian Additional Manuscripts, Royal Archives, Windsor Castle.

Privy Purse Papers.

Queen Victoria's Journal, Royal Archives, Windsor Castle.

(PP13466, PP16375, RA Add. A15/302, Vic Add. Mss U/32, RA Add. A8/1466, RA Add. A8/1468, RA Add. A8/1469, RA Add. A8/1473, RA Add. A8/1474, RA Add. A8/1475, RA Add. A8/1476, RA Add. A8/1483, PP2/93/8742, PP19833)

Letters to W. P. Frith, R.A., in the family possession.

Diary of Henry Silver, at the offices of *Punch* (unpublished manuscript).

W. P. Frith, R.A., *My Autobiography and Reminiscences*, 3 vols., (1887 & 1888)

Mrs. J. E. Panton, *Leaves from a Life* (1908)

Mrs. J. E. Panton, *More Leaves from a Life* (1911)

ed. by the Dean of Windsor and Hector Bolitho, *Letters of Lady Augusta Stanley, A Young Lady at Court 1849–1863* (1927)

The Letters of Queen Victoria, A Selection from Her Majesty's Correspondence, Second Series, 1862–85, ed by G. E. Buckle, 3 vols., (1926)

ed. by Roger Fulford, *Dearest Mama; Letters between Queen Victoria and the Crown Princess of Prussia, 1861–1864* (1968)

Henry Vizetelly, *Glances Back Through Seventy Years*, vol. 2, (1895)

Walter Sickert, *The "Derby Day"*, article in *The Burlington Magazine*, December 1922.

W. F. Monypenny and G. E. Buckle, *The Life of Benjamin Disraeli*; vol. 4, (1916)

Memories of Ernest II: Duke of Saxe-Coburg-Gotha (1890)

Arthur Ponsonby: *Henry Ponsonby, Queen Victoria's Private Secretary* (1942).

Sir Sidney Lee, *King Edward VII; a Biography* vol. 1, (1925)

Louis Blanc, *Lettres sur L'Angleterre* (1966)

ed. by Edgar Sheppard, *George Duke of Cambridge* vol. 1, (1907)

Earl of Malmesbury, *Memories of an Ex-Minister*, vol. 2, (1884)

ed. by Elliott O'Donnell, *Mrs. E. M. Ward's Reminiscences* (1911)

Reginald G. Wilberforce, *Life of Bishop Wilberforce* vol. 3, (1882)

Sir Philip Magnus, *King Edward the Seventh* (1964)

G. A. Sala, *The Life and Adventures of George Augustus Sala* (1896)

T. Matthews, *The Biography of John Gibson, R.A., Sculptor, Rome* (1911)

Vernon Heath, *Recollections* (1892)

Elizabeth Longford, *Victoria R.I.* (1964)

ed. by Sir Richard Holmes, *Edward VII, his Life and Times* vol. 1., (1910)

Roger Fulford, *The Prince Consort* (1949)

Theo Aronson, *The Coburgs of Belgium* (1968)

Theo Aronson, *The Kaisers* (1917)

W. H. Russell, *A Memorial of the Marriage of H.R.H. Albert Edward, Prince of Wales and H.R.H. Alexandra, Princess of Denmark* (n.d)

ed. by S. M. Ellis, *The Letters and Memoirs of Sir William Hardman M.A., F.R.G.S.* (1923)

Lady Login, *Sir John Login and Duleep Singh* (1890)

Alice Hughes, *My Father and I* (1923)

The Art-Journal

The Athenaeum

The Morning Post

The Times

Illustrated London News

INDEX OF NAMES